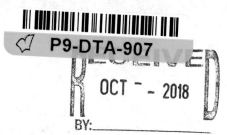
THE CHINA OPTION

A Guide for Millennials

How to Work, Play, and Find Success in China

TRAVELERS' TALES BOOKS

Country and Regional Guides

30 Days in Italy, 30 Days in the South Pacific, America, Antarctica, Australia, Brazil, Central America, China, Cuba, France, Greece, India, Ireland, Italy, Japan, Mexico, Nepal, Spain, Thailand, Tibet, Turkey; Alaska, American Southwest, Grand Canyon, Hawai'i, Hong Kong, Middle East, Paris, Prague, Provence, San Francisco, South Pacific, Tuscany

Women's Travel

100 Places Every Woman Should Go, 100 Places in Italy Every Woman Should Go, 100 Places in France Every Woman Should Go, 100 Places in Greece Every Woman Should Go, 100 Places in the USA Every Woman Should Go, 100 Places in Cuba Every Woman Should Go, 50 Places in Rome, Florence, & Venice Every Woman Should Go, Best Women's Travel Writing, Gutsy Women, Mother's World, Safety and Security for Women Who Travel, Wild with Child, Woman's Asia, Woman's Europe, Woman's Path, Woman's World, Woman's World Again, Women in the Wild

Body & Soul

Food, How to Eat Around the World,
A Mile in Her Boots, Pilgrimage, Road Within

Special Interest

Danger!, Gift of Birds, Gift of Rivers, Gift of Travel, How to Shit Around the World, Hyenas Laughed at Me, Leave the Lipstick, Take the Iguana, More Sand in My Bra, Mousejunkies!, Not So Funny When It Happened, Sand in My Bra, Testosterone Planet, There's No Toilet Paper on the Road Less Traveled, Thong Also Rises, What Color is your Jockstrap?, Wake Up and Smell the Shit, The World Is a Kitchen, Writing Away

Travel Literature

The Best Travel Writing, Soul of a Great Traveler, Deer Hunting in Paris, Fire Never Dies, Ghost Dance in Berlin, Guidebook Experiment, Kin to the Wind, Kite Strings of the Southern Cross, Last Trout in Venice, Marco Polo Didn't Go There, Rivers Ran East, Royal Road to Romance, A Sense of Place, Shopping for Buddhas, Soul of Place, Storm, Sword of Heaven, Take Me With You, Unbeaten Tracks in Japan, Way of Wanderlust, Wings, Coast to Coast

THE CHINA OPTION

A Guide for Millennials

How to Work, Play, and Find Success in China

SOPHIA ERICKSON

TRAVELERS' TALES
AN IMPRINT OF SOLAS HOUSE, INC.
PALO ALTO

Travelers' Tales and Solas House are trademarks of Solas House, Inc., Palo Alto, California. travelerstales.com | solashouse.com

Art Direction: Kimberly Nelson
Cover Design: Kimberly Nelson
Cover Photo: Maridav, Shutterstock
Interior Design and Page Layout: Howie Severson/Fortuitous Publishing

The character sprinkled throughout the book is ming. It means clear and bright, and represents the sun and the moon. It is one of the most common characters in Chinese, and combined with other characters, forms words such as 智明 cōngming (intelligent) and 明白 míngbái (understanding).

Library of Congress Cataloging-in-Publication Data is available upon request

978-1-60952-133-2 (paperback)
978-1-60952-134-9 (ebook)
978-1-60952-168-4 (hard cover))

First Edition
Printed in the United States
10 9 8 7 6 5 4 3 2 1

Contents

Introduction   vii

Why I Moved to China   xxiii

CHAPTER 1
To Beijing or Not to Beijing   1

CHAPTER 2
Hot to Get In   15

CHAPTER 3
Chinese Work Permits   41

CHAPTER 4
The Great Firewall of China   55

CHAPTER 5
Fresh off the Boeing   65

CHAPTER 6
Healthcare in China   87

CHAPTER 7
Guide to Apartment Hunting in Beijing   109

CHAPTER 8
Job Hunting in Beijing   133

CHAPTER 9
Learning Mandarin   151

CHAPTER 10
Mastering Mandarin   161

CHAPTER 11
How to Transfer Money out of China   175

CHAPTER 12
Overview of Religion in China   191

CHAPTER 13
Pollution (and Other Hazards)   213

CHAPTER 14
Travel in China   231

Photo Credits   267
Acknowledgments   269
About the Author   271

Disclaimer

I'm very frank in this book about how people of color (POC) are treated in China, and the many elements of racism that are prevalent in the country. If you are a POC reading this book, please don't dismiss moving to China out of hand as many POC do go and have extraordinary experiences; I just want to be honest about the challenges you may expect.

Introduction

SO YOU WANT TO MOVE TO CHINA

Tired of the divisive politics of the United States, scared of getting shot on your way to the super market? You want to escape, but Canada is too boring and Mexico is too dangerous.

Is it ennui? You're approaching quarter life and tired of the same old faces, same old bars, same old routines. You're stuck in a dead end job with a boss you hate and you feel vaguely cheated, slowly discovering society lied when it told you you were special and your future bright.

Or is it a sense of adventure? A desire to see the world? Life's too short to spend in a country where exotic cuisine is swapping in your white bread for whole wheat.

Maybe you want to learn Chinese. Maybe you have a passion for calligraphy, kung fu, tea, pandas, the Great Wall. Maybe you've been reading in the news that China is the up and rising superpower, Asia is the future, and you want to cash in on that.

Maybe you like Chinese girls. Maybe you feel suffocated by your tons of student debt. Maybe you're just bored. But something made you pick up this book. You want out.

The good news is you're not alone. Out is in. Every year, thousands of young foreigners just like you flock to Asia to teach English and drink cheap alcohol and take weekend trips to Thailand. And because you're not alone, the path has been paved for you. China is no longer the mysterious, forbidden kingdom of lore—so let me explain how to make your China dream come true.

FINANCIAL INCENTIVES

Ask almost anyone if they like to travel, and they will say, "Of course I would—if I had enough money." If they won the lottery they would travel, but otherwise it's just not feasible. Traveling is seen as the privilege of the elite, like a country club membership or a Lamborghini—duh, everyone would like one of those, but who can afford it?

Since money is the great stumbling block on the path to our dreams of becoming carefree gypsies, let's start by addressing the financial reasons why it makes sense to move to China.

First, let's make a straightforward comparison in terms of earning power in the U.S. versus in China. Let's look at the profile of the average Tim who moves to China: a twenty-four-year-old young graduate with a humanities degree from a mid-ranked university. According to 2014 data from the U.S. Census Bureau, Tim could expect to earn an annual salary between $25,000 to 27,000 in the U.S.

If Tim moves to China and becomes an English teacher, he can expect to make between RMB 12,000-15,000 a month in China. In terms of dollars, that's about $1,800-2,250 per month, which will add up to around $21,600 to 27,000 annually. This doesn't include the extra benefits he will receive as part of his job package — either free housing or an extra housing allowance of around RMB 2,000 per month.

Tim's gross earning power is about the same, if not slightly lower, in China as it is in the United States.

Now let's compare cost of living in the U.S. and in China (with the important caveat that there are wide disparities between different cities in both countries):

- Gross Income (Salary): 13,500 RMB
- Rent: 2500 RMB
- Utilities (electricity, gas, water): 200 RMB
- Phone & Internet: 300 RMB
- Food: 1500 RMB
- Remaining Disposable Income: 9,000 RMB ($1,350)

If Tim had stayed in the US, would he be able to save $1,350 every month while paying rent and living a nice lifestyle?

A SOLUTION FOR STUDENT LOANS

America is facing a student loans crisis. In 2016, the average American graduated with student loan debts of $35,000. Millennials cite student loans as a reason for delaying moving into their own apartment, buying a car, buying a house, getting married, and starting a family.

Student loans also have an opportunity cost — money put towards student loan repayment is taken away from retirement savings. If a fresh graduate put $35,000 in the bank from graduation until retirement, compound interest would turn the amount into $684,474 by the time he retires. Paying off your student loans young has huge repercussions on your ability to retire early and enjoy a relaxing end of life.

Teaching in China is an excellent way to pay off a large chunk of your student loan. Putting $1000 towards student loan repayment every month would still allow you to have a high standard of living while paying off your loans entirely within three years! Even if three years seems too long to spend living in China, within a year or two you could have saved up enough to make a significant dent in your loan repayment. This takes pressure off you to immediately get a high-paying job when you return to the States. Even better, you don't have to move into your parents' basement. And you get to do all this while living in a fascinating country, enjoying the world's best cuisine, and exploring the beaches of Southeast Asia. Becoming a teacher in China makes excellent financial sense for a recent graduate, and were

Millennials robots motivated by profit they would all be fighting for the chance to teach at New Oriental.

But humans are not robots. We don't always make the rational economic choice, to the frustration of economists in ivory towers across the world. Moving to China requires a certain amount of sacrifice. It's a foreign country, with an unfamiliar language and culture. It's far from home and friends and family and familiar comforts. Teaching English is not an obvious stepping stone on the path to a lucrative career.

LANGUAGE

Yet spending a year in China can help you reap rewards in different ways. For one, there's the language: Mandarin is the most widely-spoken language in the world. It is the mother tongue of 873 million people, and the official language of the most populous country in the world. China's economy is expected to surpass America's to become the largest economy in the world by 2018. As China becomes a global superpower, it is expanding its reach in Asia, Africa, and Latin America.

Learning Mandarin will unquestionably give you an edge in the world of tomorrow—and even today. China is currently the U.S.'s top trading partner, which means if you have an interest in creating a product you will be working with Mandarin-speaking manufacturers. Steve Jobs once remarked he had no choice but to make the iPhone in China as no other country could produce it at such high speed and low cost. And China isn't just a country of factories and manufacturers — as Chinese companies become richer, they are starting to expand their portfolios overseas. Alibaba recently invested $200 million in Snapchat. Dididache just bought out Uber in China.

And this is not to mention the vastness of China's consumer market. According to Forbes, the Chinese consumer market currently makes up 35 percent of sales of luxury goods internationally. Alibaba's TMall and Taobao online retail store have more active shoppers than the entire U.S. population. On a single day, November 11, 2015, Alibaba made $14.3 billion dollars of sales in less than 24 hour. As China continues to develop at breakneck speed and increase its people's spending power, the country's population gives it a center of gravity that draws the whole world in.

You might argue that many American businesses are successfully trading with China without forcing all their employees to learn Chinese. After all, English is the international language of businesses, and any contract you sign will be in the world's lingua franca. That might be true, but speaking Mandarin will give you an edge in the hypercompetitive Chinese market.

Chinese business culture rests on the concept of guanxi, which can loosely be translated as relationships. Networking and making connections is crucial to succeeding in the Chinese market, and speaking Mandarin will immediately boost your credibility with your Chinese business partners.

American companies attempting to break into the Chinese market have often remarked on this phenomenon. Tom Adams, CEO of Rosetta Stone, attributed his success in China with his ability to conduct business in Mandarin. Mark Zuckerberg received widespread admiration when he conducted a Q&A at Tsinghua University entirely in Mandarin, a feat for which Bill Gates praised him, stating his one regret in life was that he never learned a foreign language.

As China continues to expand its international influence, the ability to converse in Mandarin and conduct business on an equal footing with English-speaking Chinese will be an important advantage in conducting business internationally. For this reason alone, multinational human resources experts are encouraging young graduates to learn Mandarin as soon as possible to push their resumes to the top of the list.

The twenty-first century is the age of global interconnectedness. Speaking Mandarin gives you access to the world's largest market and increases your ability to work with America's largest trading partner. It's easier to learn a language when you're young, so invest the time now and reap the benefits for the rest of your life.

ENRICHING EXPERIENCE

For two years I worked for a company that helped Chinese students prepare to study abroad in the Anglo world. My students were young, mostly teenagers. They had grown up in provinces all across China and almost none had had the opportunity to travel within their own country, let alone abroad. When I asked them why they had chosen to take the huge leap of going overseas for university, their answer (if it was not an honest "because my parents are forcing me") was invariably some version of "To broaden my horizon. To open my mind."

This is a pretty standard response recited by anyone who wishes to travel. In the West we too are encouraged to see the world, to experience different cultures, to open our minds. Yet when I asked my students what they would gain from broadening their horizons and opening their minds, it was clear they had never considered this question before, and could rarely articulate an answer.

I couldn't blame them. Broadening your horizons and opening your mind seems such a self-evidently beneficial thing to do that it also took me a long time to wonder what exactly those nebulous concepts meant. Of course there are the quantitative benefits I listed above—learning a language, gaining professional skills, having an interesting paragraph to add to your resume. But when I look back on my time in Beijing it is not the concrete gains from which I feel I have most benefited.

Moving to China will change you. This change will not come from having the experience of sitting over a squat toilet or eating chicken feet—these are the most superficial aspects of living abroad, amusing diversions from the true lessons to be learned from a foreign culture. Living in China will change you because it will expose you to an un-Western way of thinking and viewing the world. It will make you question the core values with which you have been raised, and ultimately either reject them, or reaffirm your belief with renewed fervor, now understanding the principle behind your convictions.

For a Westerner coming to China, one such key belief is individualism. Americans and Europeans are all raised to believe in our individual selves as the center of the world. We are indoctrinated in the dogma of selfishness, told that our most important duty is the pursuit of individual happiness, that we should "be ourselves" and reject those who would block our path to personal fulfilment. Stories where the plucky hero finally stands up to his heartless parents who would come between his dream of becoming a musician and marrying the girl he loves are celebrated in our culture.

Enter Confucius. Confucius taught Chinese people they are a cog in a great communal machine, whose duty it is to perform the task that has been allocated to them to the best of their ability. Chinese children are not raised with the idea that their individuality is something to be celebrated, nor that personal happiness is in and of itself a goal worth pursuing. Obey your government, obey your parents, and find contentment in your contribution to maintaining a stable society.

This mind-set is pervasive in Chinese society. Teenagers have fully absorbed it by the time they graduate high school. Ask a Chinese student what major he will choose, and his answer will be some variation of, "My dream is to study architecture...but my parents want me to study finance, so I will study finance." Your parents disapproving of your boyfriend is seen not only as a valid reason to break up with him, but an obligation to do so. Ask a colleague if they like your arrogant, overbearing boss, and they will give you a puzzled look and say, "What do you mean? He is my boss, how can I say if I don't like him?"

Perhaps you will find you dislike this mode of thinking. You will look at your dutiful, passionless students and wish they could shake themselves up and take control of their own lives. You will pity your colleague trapped with an indifferent husband and a dreary job who seems to have very little to live for in this life. Westerners often leave China with a renewed appreciation for our culture, which celebrates passion and creativity and individualism.

And yet we also leave feeling like we have learned something from this communal mind-set. Chinese people are very generous. My students were constantly buying each other snacks and treats, never expecting to be repaid. If one of them was sick or struggled with answering a question, there would always be a classmate to step up and volunteer assistance. In a Chinese restaurant, everyone orders dishes for the whole table and shares everything. Your friends will show affection by picking the best bits from each dish and putting them on your plate, and then fight for the privilege of paying the bill. They wonder why foreigners always say please and thank you, as they consider doing small favors for each other so natural that there is no need to express gratitude.

Chinese who have been abroad comment that in the West, people treat strangers like family and family like strangers — Westerners are more friendly to strangers than a Chinese would be, but they treat their family with a distance and indifference that seem callous to someone with Confucian values. They find it strange that Westerners entering adulthood feel ashamed if they have to live with their parents or ask them for money. They are shocked by the treatment of the elderly, who are left to live by themselves with only their TV set as entertainment before being shipped off to a retirement home when they are too weak to care for themselves. In China, old people can be spotted dancing and singing in the street, playing mah-jong, taking their grandchildren for a walk around the park before returning to the home they still share with their children.

Westerners could learn a thing or two from this selflessness and communal spirit. We could also learn from the Chinese work ethic, their discipline with money, their willingness to sacrifice short-term pleasure for long-term benefit. When I say that China has broadened my horizon and opened my mind, I am referring both to the renewed appreciation it gave me for my own culture as well as the flaws it revealed.

And living in China will not only expose you to Chinese culture — it will expose you to the hundreds of other foreigners who will be living and working alongside you. Germans, Swedes, French, Russians, Pakistanis, Eritreans, Cameroonians, South Africans, Koreans, Japanese, Mexicans, Colombians: Beijing and Shanghai are cultural melting pots in the true sense of the word. Expats bond over the experience of living in a culture whose foreignness dwarfs our differences and we intermix to an extent rarely seen in our home countries.

Living in China not only gives you a different perspective on your own society, it also lets you see yourself in a new light. China is undeniably a harsh environment. There are days when you will feel that the air is unbreathable, the food is toxic, the crowds are claustrophobic, the language is incomprehensible, the people are bizarre. How will you respond to adversity?

Sadly, some foreigners joke that coming to China has turned them racist. They respond to the obstacles they face in living and working with Chinese people with bitterness and an endless stream of cynicism and complaints.

Others find that, away from the eyes of friends and family and long-term repercussions, they go a little bit wild. With money to blow and time to kill, they can go out and get smashed every night of the week, taking advantage of the naïveté of Chinese girls to supply them with a steady stream of sexual partners.

Others rise to the challenge, learning Mandarin, building strong friendships with Chinese people, making connections that will help them advance their careers, adjusting smoothly to the new world in which they find themselves.

Transplanting yourself to a country where you don't know anyone and must live in difficult circumstances with a lot of personal freedom can be character-revealing. If you've spent your life in your hometown, with parents always close by to take care of you, comfortable in a familiar environment and never having to face any significant difficulties, moving to China will help you see what you're made of. A year in China is a maturing experience. To paraphrase the enduring words of Disney's Hua Mulan, "[China] will make a man out of you!"

Living in China can also be a revealing experience for those who have never been a minority in our own countries. I am not trying to equate the experience of being black in America to being white in China—for the most part in China whiteness is a source of respect and privilege, which is totally opposite the minority experience in America.

But it's interesting to suddenly find you are the only white person in the room, and your behaviour is held representative of everyone of your race and nationality. Chinese will constantly ask you, "What do Americans think about the NBA? What do Americans think about Jay Chou? What do Americans think about the Communist Party?" as if you can telepathically know what the three hundred million plus people in your home country feel about any given issue. Your individuality will be eroded. Tell someone you don't like basketball and they will nod sagely and say, "Ah yes, Americans don't like basketball." Alternatively, they will give you a puzzled look and say, "But all Americans like basketball! You must like basketball too." Everything you say and do will be scrutinized not in the context of you as an individual being, but as a representative of your people.

Sometimes you will have to deal with the negative preconceptions Chinese people have about your people. White men with Chinese girlfriends report being harassed on the street by Chinese men who believe foreigners are stealing their women. Occasionally you will encounter the hostile taxi driver who hates you because of something your government has done over which you have absolutely no control. There are stories of white foreigners being beat up on the street after the disputes over the South China Sea Islands.

Being a foreigner in China means you will be continuously stared at, stereotyped, and held to a higher standard of behaviour than the locals. While this is not comparable to the difficulties minorities face in their home countries, it can be an eye-opening experience for someone who has always enjoyed the privilege of being part of the majority group.

LIFESTYLE

Yet perhaps the most compelling reason for a millennial to move to China is that it's fun. Where else in the world can a twenty-something travel around the postcard-ready beaches of South East Asia, eat at nice restaurants, take taxis everywhere, live in a nice apartment, and have maid service, while still paying off student loans?

If you're going to be working a boring, dead end job — why not do it in a country where every day feels like an adventure? When you walk out the door and see the world brimming with potential discoveries? Encountering concepts and ideas that will challenge everything you believed to be true? Grow some skills that could eventually help you in your career? Have experiences that make you grow as a person, that increase your understanding of the world, that make you grow wiser and tougher? China is as close to another planet as we will find in this world — why not experience something completely alien?

Life is short. Make it count.

Why I Moved to China

Some are born in China, some go to China, and some have China thrust upon them. I was in the third category.

After graduating at twenty-one, I spent the summer in my grandparents' house on Cape Cod. I had no clear idea what I wanted to do, and vaguely felt like I was too young to get one of those adult banking and consulting jobs all my peers seemed to be flocking to. But I wasn't free to do anything more exciting: soon I had to start paying student loans that would severely limit my options. So I drifted about for a few months, waitressing to procrastinate having to make a decision about my future.

Out of the blue, a Chinese friend from high school I had sporadically kept in touch with over the years sent me a message: "I have a job opportunity for you! Do you want to work for my father'scompany as an English teacher? It's a good company and he will pay well."

In a panic I called my parents to debate what I should do. They thought the job would be a good addition to my CV and a fun thing to do as a post-university gap year. I had studied Mandarin in high school, though I had never been particularly dedicated and in the three intervening years I had forgotten everything. Spending a year in China would get me speaking Mandarin again so the idea had a sort of surface logic.

The author during her first week in China, having second thoughts about the wisdom of her decision.

I asked my friend more details about the position. It turned out the job she had in mind would be online—consulting via Skype—but since I had shown interest in moving to Beijing, with her usual efficiency she had talked to her father and he had created a job in his company for me. After she made all that effort for me I felt obligated to go. A month later I was at LAX waiting for my flight to Beijing.

My parents still tease me about how scared I looked as I boarded my Air China plane. I tell them I was right to be terrified, and had I known what the next three months would bring I would have been more terrified still.

Adjusting to Beijing was tough. I loved the food but it seemed to be an unrequited love: I was constantly sick, and spent many long minutes getting intimately acquainted with Chinese squat toilets. I couldn't figure out basic things like how to buy shampoo since I couldn't communicate with any of the shop attendants. I was the only non-Chinese in my company, and most of my colleagues spoke about two words of English. I spoke about four words of Mandarin myself, and our six common words made for limited conversation since two of them were "yes" and "no." Because I was new, my boss gave me the lowest-level classes. These were the students who were profoundly indifferent to learning English, and teaching them was not dissimilar to teaching a brick wall.

My professional life was a disaster, and my personal life wasn't much better. I was used to living in an environment where making friends was a matter of showing up to where I was supposed to be every morning. Though my colleagues and I did not speak the same language, I thought they could smile or make some effort to display friendliness, but they hardly acknowledged my presence. Later on I realized they probably did want to talk to me but were too shy to approach the foreigner. At the time they just seemed rude. I decided that all Chinese people were rude, and spent most of my free time lying in bed, alternately feeling sorry for myself or angrily wondering how I could ever have been stupid and arrogant enough to think this was a good idea.

Wallowing in self-pity is one way to kill a few months, but eventually it gets boring. After a while I decided couldn't spend a whole year lying in bed, so I picked myself up and started to look around. I ventured out of my work bubble to explore the rich and vibrant city of Beijing. I started to understand how to navigate the cultural differences between me and my students and mended our relations until I looked forward to teaching them each day. I befriended the other expats stupid and arrogant enough to have thought moving to China was a good idea (and learned that the nice word for "stupid and arrogant" is adventurous), and slowly I began to have the best time of my life.

I hope this guide will help others skip the lying in bed crying part of the story, and move straight into having a blast, because China is filled with rich and exciting opportunities for anyone bold enough to seek them.

明

CHAPTER 1

To Beijing or Not to Beijing

﹡

You might be sold on the benefits of teaching English in China, but the question remains which city to move to. China is a vast country with a huge diversity of geography and climates. If you like tropical beaches, Hainan's turquoise water and white sand will sound appealing. If you prefer deserts and mountain ranges, you will be drawn to Western provinces like Gansu and Xinjiang. How to pick?

Chinese cities are usually divided into different tiers. The distinction between these tiers can be murky as different people have different classification systems, but essentially more developed cities are lower on the tier ladder than less developed cities. There are approximately four or five tiers, depending on whom you ask.

It is generally accepted that Tier 1 is Beijing and Shanghai. These are highly developed international cities with excellent infrastructure and a large expat community. Expats like first tier cities because in addition to providing more career opportunities, they have recognizable Western brands, chain restaurants and even supermarkets. Beijing has Carrefour, Ikea, Starbucks, McDonald's, and KFC as far as the eye can see, and even boasts its very own Hooters!

CHINESE SUPERMARKETS

Good supermarket selection might not seem like a glamorous reason to move to a city, but you will be grateful for your Carrefour when you arrive in the summer and desperately seek some deodorant, but find it completely absent in any Chinese shop since Chinese people don't use it (and don't worry, they smell fine — we are the stinky ones who need it).

Also missing in most Chinese supermarkets: floss, tampons, makeup, and other basic Western household items.

LIFE IN THE THIRD TIER

In cities like Shenying or Harbin where white faces are rare, you will be bombarded with job offers, repeatedly invited to parties and events in order to give your host face, and generally treated like a Z list celebrity-zoo animal hybrid. Children will point and stare, strangers will want to take a picture with you, and a chorus of "Hello's!" will follow you wherever you go.

Tier 1 cities also have vibrant nightlife, which is still an underdeveloped industry in smaller Chinese cities. China traditionally doesn't have any bars, and Chinese shops offer only either beer-flavored water or baijiu, which tastes like and feels similar to drinking gasoline. But Western-style revelry has started to spill into the Middle Kingdom, and Tier 1 cities now have their own nightclubs, craft beers, breweries, wine shops, and cocktail bars in most central neighborhoods. There are also many foreigners to mingle with and meet and greet. If you have good networking skills you could eventually transition from ESL to working for a large multinational company and give your resume an additional shine.

Tier 1 cities have their disadvantages — they are consistently plagued with the worst traffic in the world, large crowds and pollution. An excess of expats could be seen as a negative — it can be easy to isolate yourself in an expat bubble and spend little time interacting with Chinese culture or learning Mandarin. Yet you can choose to avoid this, as there are certainly enough Chinese people in Beijing's thirty million-plus population for you to find one or two to befriend.

Expats in Tier 2+ cities report that their foreignness is a greater source of privilege outside the first tier. Some expats enjoy the feeling of being treated like royalty despite their profound mediocrity, and these cities can attract the narcissistic weirdoes who give ESL teachers a bad reputation. The

THIRD TIER: TWILIGHT ZONE

Alexa spent 8 months living in Linyi, a city in Shandong province, before moving to Beijing. Her experience was typical of what I've heard from other expats in third-tier cities:

The first thing you have to understand is that in a city like Linyi, you can't choose your friends. If you don't speak Mandarin you have no choice but to hang out with the other expats, even if you would never associate with people like them back home.

I became close friends with two of my co-workers: Jim and John. Both were American. They were nice guys but they had issues. Jim turned out to be a crack addict, and John drank so much he got ulcers and was frequently in pain.

Our social circle had many foreign boys who suffered from "white god complex": They get used to Chinese girls going crazy over them, and have a different Chinese girl on their arm every night. Occasionally they got one pregnant and had to pay for her abortion.

Will and Mike were particularly notorious in this regard. They would brag that they could have sex with three different girls in one night. They had no respect for the different cultural expectations around sex in China — on several occasions one of them took a girl's virginity and when she found out he had no intentions of marrying her she became hysterical and even violent. Eventually their reputation got so bad that a group of Chinese men ganged up on them outside a nightclub and beat them up.

We all hung out in a bar owned by a Chinese guy we called "Tiger," who was a prominent businessman in town. He always wore a backwards baseball cap and had an entourage that consisted of two bodyguards and young attractive Chinese girls. He invited foreigners to drink at his bar, and conducted his business in the corner while we danced nearby, presumably using us as a backdrop to gain face.

Tiger frequently invited all the expats to banquets with other Chinese businessmen. We would eat sumptuous feasts and the men would drink baijiu until they were puking on the floor while the Chinese spoke in Mandarin and basically ignored us. One day, Tiger told Jim that he was a human trafficker, and bragged about the beautiful women he caught in Southeast Asian countries. I'm not sure if that was true but I heard from several sources that Tiger was

(continued)

in the mafia. It was a very weird environment over-all, there were a lot of shady and unstable characters. An Irish guy tried to kill himself by downing a bottle of pills when he was rejected by another expat. At a banquet, a Chinese girl lit a whole pack of cigarettes and then put them out on her tongue, for reasons unknown to us. There was a Russian man who would get violent over the most trivial things, like someone saying they had a phobia of needles.

When my contract ended I moved to Beijing, and I haven't looked back. Living in Linyi was like being in the Twilight zone.

expat communities there are small and claustrophobic, and if you don't like your fellow ESL teachers it will be hard to avoid them in the town's single bar. There are exceptions, of course — many laowai move to third tier cities because they are passionate about learning Mandarin and integrating into Chinese culture, and want to avoid the expat bubble altogether.

Ultimately I recommend living in a Tier 1 city unless you really want to immerse yourself in Chinese culture and learn Mandarin as quickly as possible. Deep China sounds nice in theory, but the culture shock is severe and expats in these cities often end up feeling bitter and alienated. A city like Beijing or Shanghai has all the allure of China without as many of the aggravations.

BEIJING OR SHANGHAI?

Beijing and Shanghai can roughly be compared to Washington DC and New York City. Beijing is the political heart of China, while Shanghai was traditionally the business and economic powerhouse. Shanghai bills itself as China's coolest and most cosmopolitan city, while Beijingers take pride in their city's more than 3,000 years of history. The two cities have been rivals for the past two hundred years, and a local from each could give a lengthy discourse on why their hometown is the best place to live.

I will summarize why Beijing is best for four simple reasons:

1. **Iconic.** While Beijing lacks Shanghai's futuristic skyline, it more than makes up for it with its iconic architecture. When you think of China, what pops into your head? For most people, the answer is the Great Wall, Tiananmen Square, and the Forbidden City, all of which can be found in Beijing. Three thousand years of history have left Beijing a legacy of stunning temples, one of the oldest mosques in the world, and blocks of beautiful traditional

Pick your iconic building: the Pants or the Pearl?

THE ROSETTA STONE: CHINGLISH EDITION

Chinglish (portmanteau of Chinese and English)

Chinglish is the bastard love child of English and Mandarin. A mongrel language riddled with improper grammar and cryptic turn of phrases intelligible only to Chinese English speakers, and expats in China.

E.g. "When I started teaching ESL I thought my students' English would improve; instead mine got worse and now we all speak Chinglish."

courtyard houses. By contrast, Shanghai was little more than a fishing village two hundred years ago and lacks the unique historic appeal of China's capital.

2. **Language.** Beijing is undeniably a better place to learn Mandarin than Shanghai. The most obvious reason is that the local dialect of Shanghai is Shanghainese, whereas the only dialect in Beijing is Mandarin. Of course all Chinese must learn Mandarin at school so any Shanghai person will be able to speak it, but you will not be surrounded by it constantly, as is the case in Beijing. It is also

a well-known phenomenon that Shanghai people speak better English than Beijingers, perhaps because the city has a much higher concentration of foreigners. Moreover, while Shanghai people prefer to speak English to foreigners even when the expat speaks excellent Mandarin, the reverse is true in Beijing — Beijingers much prefer to converse in Chinese even if their English is better than your Mandarin.

3. **University.** Beijing is the educational powerhouse of China. While Shanghai has Fudan, Beijing has Tsinghua, Peking, BLCU, and dozens more of China's top universities. This makes Beijing the most popular destination for foreigners seeking to learn Mandarin. It also draws a large number of intellectuals, international political leaders and business moguls, and artists. Within the two-year stretch when I lived in China, Beijingers were presented with the opportunity to attend speeches by Mark Zuckerberg (which he conducted in Mandarin), Angela Merkel, Ai Weiwei, and more. Shanghai simply does not present as many opportunities to meet and discuss with the world's leading intellectuals.

4. **Expats.** Maybe I'm a little biased, but I find that generally Beijing expats are a more interesting lot than their Shanghai counterparts. Beijingers came to China with an interest in the language and culture. They are hardier and more adventurous, willing to brave bouts of suffocatingly dense smog, freezing Mongolian winds and dust storms on

EXPATS WEIGH IN: WHY CHINA?

The author surveyed expats she met in Shanghai and in Beijing to ask the reason they moved to China.

Shanghai expats most frequently cited Shanghai's party scene, lifestyle, party, shopping, party, travel, and most importantly: party.

Beijing expats cited desire to learn about Chinese history, language, culture, and business practices.

This highly scientific study conclusively proves that Beijing expats are more ambitious, intellectual, interesting, smart, and generally better than Shanghai expats.

(or maybe we are just more arrogant)

their way to work. Shanghai expats came to China because they heard it has a nice party scene, and they are content as long as they have a steady supply of French cheese and rum. There's also too many of them — walk down the street in Xuhui and you might as well be somewhere in Europe. Even the waiters are white. If you want to live in Europe, move to Berlin. Beijing offers a more authentically Chinese experience.

Beijing is the best place for foreigners to move in China. It is a highly developed international city that remains authentically Chinese, though not too authentic. It's a great place to learn Mandarin and meet a variety of interesting people.

明

CHAPTER TWO

How To Get In

There are several channels through which you can enter China. You can choose to study there, either through an American program or by enrolling directly at a Chinese university. Both of these are expensive.

You can also get a working visa that will allow you to work in jobs outside of education—but these jobs are extremely competitive. Ten years ago having a white face and native English could get your foot in the door at any Chinese company, but those days are long gone. Now unless you speak basic Mandarin and possess some skills in high demand (think engineer, IT) odds are you will not be able to get a regular office job. Chinese companies don't want to hire a foreigner when a local could do a better job at one-third of the salary.

Yet there is still one golden ticket into China—teaching English, a career which must have the most favorable ratio in the world when it comes to skill vs. salary. Virtually any English speaker can get a job as an English teacher, which will allow you to work short hours and maintain a standard of living in the top first percentile of the country. That's

QUICK FACTS ABOUT CHINA'S ESL INDUSTRY

In 2015, Chinese Vice Premier Lui Yandong stated that more than 300 million Chinese were actively pursuing English lessons

Britain's Guardian newspaper estimated that there are at least 30,000 companies in China offering private English lessons.

In 2015, the ESL industry in China was worth $4.4 billion.

right: You can be the 1% of the biggest country in the world with no skills and few working hours.

China has an insatiable demand for foreign teachers and getting a job in this field essentially entails showing up. You don't necessarily have to speak great English either — the country is filled with thickly-accented Russians and Ukrainians singing the ABCs to kindergarteners.

A note on race: China has never gone through anything resembling a civil rights movement, and people here are openly racist. If you are not white this might translate into lower salary and difficulty getting hired, though a Western passport and American or English accent can help compensate for skin color. There are plenty of black British or American English teachers in China, but white skin is undeniably an asset in this country (see "Racism" on page 126).

So how does one get a teaching job?

BASIC QUALIFICATIONS TO TEACH LEGALLY

Teaching legally means that you have obtained a Z-visa or Foreign Expert Certificate and are officially allowed to work in China. If you want to be 100% safe and play by the rules, here are the criteria you must meet:

1. Native English speaker from the United States, United Kingdom, Australia, Canada, South Africa, or New Zealand. You must have a passport from one of these countries.

2. You must have a bachelor's degree.

3. Additionally, you must have two years of postgraduate work experience. Some exceptions are made if you have a master's degree in education or related field or one year's teaching experience, but you need to check with the visa agent.

4. Between 24-55 years of age (24 is not set in stone, but in order to meet the two years postgraduate work experience, most will be this age).

5. Many schools also demand a TEFL (Teaching English as a Foreign Language) certificate, though this is not a requirement for the visa itself.

(This is according to the most recent guidelines on obtaining a Foreign Expert or Z Visa certificate. Keep in mind that these rules are frequently changed and updated.)

Don't meet these criteria? You're not alone. It is difficult to obtain exact statistics on what percentage of teachers

NON-NATIVE ENGLISH TEACHERS

Only native speakers of English can be issued teaching visas. Yet TEFL is the most lucrative career for foreigners in China, and non-native speakers find ways to get around the restrictions.

The author was puzzled to meet two New Jersey girls with bizarre accents and grammar patterns at a pre-school English company. After class they admitted they were really Russians trying to pass for Americans by imitating the speech patterns of the stars of Jersey Shore.

Likewise with an "Irish" co-worker, who turned out to be a Serbian in disguise.

in China are working legally, but personal experience and anecdotal evidence suggests it is quite low. Many schools cannot be bothered with the bureaucratic nightmare that is Chinese visa application and will turn a blind eye to your tourist visa, and most of the time there are no consequences. If you look at job classifieds websites like echinacities.com, you will see many teaching positions that advertise "no work visa required, and doesn't have to be native speaker!" It is up to you whether you are willing to take the risk of a hefty fine and deportation. This rarely happens but it is a possibility, and the risk has been rising in recent years as the Chinese government has been cracking down on illegal teachers.

HOW TO FIND A JOB

Assuming that you meet the criteria to obtain a work permit, here is how to go about finding a job.

First of all, beware scammers. There are many unscrupulous companies in China whose business model rests on the old adage, "A fool and his money are soon parted." They will ask you to send them money to pay for training and materials before you can begin earning a salary.

You are the employee. You should be receiving money, not giving it to your boss.

Trust your intuition—if a company rings your alarm bells, move along. And use your common sense. If something seems too good to be true, it probably is. If an unknown

---

CAUTIONARY TALE

An American was offered a high-paying job for a training company in China. They promised him a steady stream of fabulously wealthy clients if he would only pay for the expensive textbook upfront.

"Can't you take it out of my salary?" he asked.

"Impossible."

"Why?"

"Company policy."

Hmmm.

---

company is offering you a starting salary of RMB25,000 per month, when a similar position at a reputable institution like New Oriental offers only RMB13,000, beware.

A quick Google search of your company name along with "scam" might turn up results, so make sure to do your research before signing any contracts. Foreigners in China are highly vulnerable and often cannot access the protection of the law (to be fair the same could be said of Chinese people in China). Be smart.

Feeling intimidated? The good news is there are many well-established, reputable venues through which you can enter China. You can take two routes.

SCAM ALERT

A company hires you from the USA. Salary is excellent, you are offered free housing and flights home, and promised short working hours. Happily you accept and buy your plane ticket.

When you arrive, your boss makes excuses as to why you need to work twice as many hours as you were told earlier. There are also reasons why your salary is late or diminished—your performance is poor, you must go through a three-month trial period before earning full pay, the bank is on holiday, your boss's phone has been eaten by a crocodile and he is unable to take any of your calls, and so on. End result is you're making half as much as you were promised and there is nothing you can do about it.

Some of the particularly nefarious institutions will make you put down a large deposit when you sign the contract (under the pretext that they have had bad experiences with foreigners vanishing unexpectedly without giving notice), and you will then feel obligated to fulfill your full contract or risk losing all your money. The practice has undertones of indentured servitude.

1. Find a placement company in the United States that will
   sponsor you to go to China. Some of the biggest companies are English First, New Oriental, Wall Street English,
   and Gold Star English, but there are hundreds. The benefit of going through a company is that you can be secure
   you will have a job and lodgings waiting for you when
   you step off the plane exhausted and disoriented after a

> I met a British girl with a heavy scouse accent at a bar
> in Beijing. The girl was drinking forlornly by herself
> and we invited her to join our group. She told us she
> had come from India where she had been backpack-
> ing for several months. Her funds had run low and
> she was dreading the prospect of calling her parents
> to ask them to buy her a ticket home.
>
> We laughed at her despair and reassured her that
> all a blond girl with a British passport needed to do
> to get a job in Beijing was snap her fingers. We wrote
> down the name of two popular job-seeking websites
> on a napkin and sent her on her way.
>
> Within three days she found a job as a Kindergarten
> teacher making RMB 13,000 a month. She took the
> job for a few months and then continued on her
> merry way across Asia.

fourteen-hour flight. Beware, however, that some companies will take up to one-third of your salary every month
in exchange for finding you a placement. For that reason,
some people prefer to go the second route.

2. Come to China and apply directly to a school here. A website like echinacities will yield thousands upon thousands
of job opportunities for English teaching, and you will get
to keep all your pay. As long as you meet the requirements
for a work permit, you are almost guaranteed to quickly
find a job. Yet you will also have to deal with the uncer-
tainty of moving to Beijing without any support system to
help you find an apartment and navigate Chinese life. This
is the option for the more adventurous.

Assuming you are a stereotypical laowai English teacher
(no teaching experience, no relevant degree, graduated
from a university Chinese people are unlikely to know) here
is what you can expect from a job in China:

• **Salary:** RMB13k to 17k per month is standard in one of the
major cities like Beijing, Shanghai, or Guangzhou. If you
convert this into US dollars it doesn't seem like much, but
considering the median salary for a middle class Chinese
in these cities is 6000 RMB/month it is actually excellent
pay. You can expect to fork out RMB2-3k for monthly
rent and the rest goes in your pocket. Other than rent,
cost of living is extremely low. As long as you don't spend

THE ROSETTA STONE
CHINGLISH EDITION

Laowai (老外, pinyin: lɑ̀owài, lit. "old foreign")

Slang term for foreigner. Commonly used by Chinese and expats alike.

E.g. "I am so sick of Chinese people charging me laowai prices when they hear me speak English!"

all your nights out drinking your money away, you can expect to save between $10,000 to $15,000 every year.

- **Benefits:** Some companies will offer to pay for your air-fare home once a year. Some companies will also give you a lodging stipend and pay for your Chinese classes. It depends on the company.
- **Holiday:** You will have all Chinese national holidays, and many companies allow you to take extra weeks off during the Chinese New Year and summer holidays. Again, this depends on the company. Most English teachers I know spend at least a month of the year traveling around Southeast Asia or going home, as well as frequent short trips during the year.

THE ROSETTA STONE
CHINGLISH EDITION

Gaokao (高考, pinyin: gāo kαo, lit. "High Test")

China's National Higher Education Entrance Examination

The Gaokao is China's national college entrance examination. Anyone who wants to attend a Chinese university must take this exam, and it is essentially the sole criteria for college admissions.

China is a Confucian country that places a high premium on education, and this culture in combination with the largest population in the world make the Gaokao absurdly competitive. It looms large in the life of every Chinese student, who prepares for it essentially from first grade.

The Gaokao has a major influence on how Chinese students study English. It tests only reading and writing, so many Chinese neglect the listening and speaking aspect of language learning. If you teach children who have not yet graduated high school, you can expect Gaokao preparation to be a large part of your curriculum.

E.g. "I didn't do very well on the Gaokao. Guess I'll be a janitor for the rest of my life."

TYPES OF SCHOOLS

Learning English is big business in China. English used to be a huge part of the Gaokao, and all Chinese begin studying in English in first grade. The government has recently decreased the importance of English in the exam, but everyone continues to study English. Speaking the world's lingua franca is seen as a mark of worldliness and prestige, and many young Chinese students dream of studying abroad in the Anglo world. English teaching is therefore a huge industry, and in a country with a 1.4 billion rapidly developing population, there is tons of money to be made. Here are the kinds of school where you can expect to teach:

Cram Schools

Biggest players: New Oriental, English First, Wall Street English

The purpose of these schools is to make money, and they do this by promising students higher scores on standardized tests like the Gaokao, TOEFL, and IELTS

Pros: small classes, high pay, no need to come up with personal material

Cons: can be a soul-sucking exercise in test-taking. Since parents are paying for the education they must be satisfied with the result—this can sometimes lead to sacrificing quality of teaching for being an entertainer who keeps the students happy, or on the other hand pushing the students too hard to make progress resulting in their being bored and exhausted.

Public schools

Public schools all around Beijing look for foreigners to teach their students English. Beijing public schools tend to have very large class sizes (30-50), and the students face intense pressure to succeed on the Gaokao.

Pros: stable 9-5 hours, long holidays, easy to get hired.

Cons: low pay, very large classes, students are stressed and facing immense pressure to succeed on the Gaokao.

Contemplating life as a janitor if he fails his exam.

"Working for New Oriental is like being a chef at McDonald's. You have to feed your client the same pre-packaged s*** each time or you get fired."

— Disgruntled former employee of New Oriental

Private schools

China's education system is different from many Western systems in that private schools are generally considered worse than public schools — they are for rich children whose scores were too low to get into a top public school. Yet there are many excellent international schools in Beijing that target students who want to go study abroad in the US, UK, or Australia. These students generally speak excellent English as their whole education has been in the language.

Pros: high salary, stable 9-5 hours, high-level students, will often provide housing.

Cons: private schools often have higher standards for the foreign teachers they hire. You will definitely need a TEFL certificate, and if you did not study education in the US you will need to demonstrate previous teaching experience.

Kindergarten

Chinese parents like to give their children a head start by making them study English almost as soon as they start speaking. Kindergartens are among the top employers of foreign teachers as parents are willing to shell out a lot of money to ensure their little darling is ahead of the curve when he starts first grade.

Pros: highest salary for English teachers, low requirement to get hired, stable 9-5 job, long holidays, kids are photogenic and easily generate dozens of Instagram likes.

Cons: these kids will literally not speak a word of English when you meet them (older students will all have been exposed to English since at least first grade), trying to control thirty overactive kids who don't understand anything you say is not everyone's idea of a good time, other expats regard foreign kindergarten teachers as the bottom of the totem pole since the bar to get hired is so low.

University

All universities in Beijing are looking for foreign teachers for their English departments. These jobs are the most competitive since being a university professor is considered more prestigious than teaching kindergarteners. You will probably need a master's degree. Beijing Language and

Culture University (BLCU) in particular hires a large number of foreigners, and they don't always require a master's degree.

Pros: a lot of flexibility with your curriculum, students are more mature and engaged since they are choosing to study English, stable 9-5 job, very long paid holidays (up to 5 months a year!), free housing, prestige.

Cons: low salary—don't expect to make more than 8000-10000 RMB a month. The free housing compensates for this, however, since it's essentially saving you 3000 RMB/month.

Business English Schools

Most of the schools mentioned above target young Chinese students. Yet there is also a market for graduates and professionals who are seeking to improve their English, either to promote their career or as a hobby.

Pros: small class sizes, students choose to be there so are more engaged, students are more mature and confident so it's easier to draw them into interesting conversations.

Cons: pay is lower than for teaching kids (Chinese parents are willing to spend a lot of money on their children but not on themselves), classes are scheduled in the evenings and weekends.

Private Lessons

Rich Chinese families will sometimes hire foreigners to act as aux pair/English teachers for their child.

Pros: pay tends to be very high, you will get to live in a nice house, intimate exposure to Chinese family life and culture.

Cons: can be isolating to live in a family without anyone your age or who speaks your language, lack of freedom to go about as you please and set your own schedule.

FACE

One of the more nebulous concepts of Chinese society is the idea of mianzi (面子), or face. This is one of the core social principles a foreigner must grasp in order to understand China. It permeates every aspect of interpersonal relationships in the Middle Kingdom, and behaviors that appear baffling at first glance can be understood quickly through the prism of keeping face.

Keeping face essentially means building your reputation and presenting a good front to society. When I first came to China I did not understand why people talked about face as if it were a unique quality of Chinese society—doesn't everyone in the world care at least to some extent about what others think? Humans are vain creatures, simultaneously arrogant and insecure, needy of their community's approval. Why did Chinese people think they were special because they had a name for this universal behavior?

THE ROSETTA STONE
CHINGLISH EDITION

Middle Kingdom (中国 , pinyin: Zhōngguó, lit: central nation)

The Mandarin word for China can be loosely translated to Middle Kingdom, and people familiar with China often refer to it by that name when writing in English.

E.g. "Just got back from a holiday to the Middle Kingdom!"

Over time I came to realize that while there is nothing unique about the desire to look good in front of others, the extent to which China takes this behavior is unusual. The concept of "face" in China manifests itself in two ways: (1) self-consciously hierarchical behavior, and (2) a paralyzing fear of public embarrassment.

No one will be surprised to hear that China is a hierarchical country—hierarchy has been an entrenched part of the culture since Confucius made a coherent ideology out of the concept more than 2,000 years ago.

You can clearly see this hierarchy during Chinese business meetings, which consists mostly of the Big Boss talking for an hour straight while everyone listens quietly. Perhaps the underlings will occasionally answer a question or make a comment, but it will never be to question or disagree with the boss's words. To question the Boss would cause him to lose face, and he would probably retaliate by seeking opportunities to criticize you and make you lose face. In China, never question or criticize in public—save that for private conversations.

Rank is extremely important. In an office environment, you need to be aware of the managerial ladder, and always treat people with respect appropriate for the position. The Big Boss must be favored with special recognition. Buy him gifts, pay him compliments, make a toast to him during business dinners. Special treatment will give him face, and he will respond by treating you favorably and praising you, which will give you face. To behave in this way in China is not seen as obsequious or fake. Failing to treat the manager as a superior will cause him to lose face, and this could have negative repercussions for the offender.

Foreigners in Chinese office environments are to some degree exempt from the hierarchy. A foreigner will be treated with respect by his Chinese colleagues even if he is a simple English teacher at the bottom of the totem pole. Moreover, if a foreigner fails to treat the managers with appropriate respect, some leeway is given with the understanding that foreigners don't understand Chinese culture. But if you do respect the rules of face-giving, you will stand out from other foreigners and might even earn some face of your own!

The second way in which face manifests itself is a paralyzing fear of public embarrassment. This will cause Chinese people to move heaven and earth to avoid ever having to admit ignorance or wrongdoing or even inability, no matter if the mistake was innocent or the demand unreasonable.

For example, I once listened to a friend's discussion with a carpenter over a broken doorway. She asked him if he would be able to fix it by the end of the day.

"It will be difficult."

"But can you do it?"

"I will have to find the material quickly."

"I can pay extra."

"Yes, I suppose I can do it."

Satisfied, she escorted him out. "He won't do it," her Chinese roommate remarked when she came back. We asked her how she knew. "I know. He didn't tell you because he was afraid of losing face." But he said he could, we argued. If it was impossible why wouldn't he just tell us? She shrugged, and sure enough the carpenter was not able to complete the work until the next week. To a Chinese person, his hesitation would have been interpreted as a clear no. But we were oblivious foreigners, and the signaling flew over our head.

I could also see it in my interactions with my students. "If you don't understand something or don't know the answer, just tell me and I will explain better," I would beg them again and again. "It's not your fault if you don't understand; it just shows me I need to be clearer."

CHINESE DIRECTNESS VS. INDIRECTNESS

When I first arrived in China I was struck by how blunt Chinese people are.

I asked my boss on the first day if she liked her colleagues.

"A few of them I like. Most I don't like. They are colleagues."

"Do you like working for this company?"

"Not really. It's just a job."

My colleagues all said similar things. At first I wondered what kind of godforsaken company I had landed in if no one could even pretend to like their job in front of a new hire.

After having similar conversations with Chinese people for a few months, and being told repeatedly that I was too fat and had too many freckles to get a boyfriend, I accepted that Chinese people didn't feel the need to sugarcoat their words when they spoke. I would need to grow a thicker skin or spend the next year nursing my bruised ego.

So I was surprised to talk to a Chinese woman who had recently come back from a business trip to the

United States. I asked her how it went. Her: It was wonderful! I like America very much!

Me: What was so great about it?

Her: Americans are so honest and straightforward! It is so different from China!

Me: Really? How so?

Her: In America, if a company can't do business with you they will tell you directly. It is so refreshing. Not like in China.

Americans and Chinese have different ideas about when it is important to be honest vs. when it is acceptable to lie.

"We will tell you, teacher," they promised, but they never did. No one would ever say outright that they could not understand or did not know the answer. To do so would mean loss of face. Over time I learned that if my words were met with silence and averted eyes, I needed to explain myself better.

This lack of straightforwardness can be frustrating when dealing with Chinese people, especially considering how direct they are regarding other topics (You are so fat! You need to lose weight!). It is a different style of communication and takes getting used to. Understand that in China, reading someone's body language and expressions is as important as listening to their words in order to understand the message they want to convey.

Face is a pervasive aspect of Chinese society. It is difficult for foreigners to fully grasp it at first, but follow these three basic rules and you should be able to navigate Chinese society successfully enough:

1. Never criticize someone in front of others.
2. Be aware of the hierarchy of your office environment, and treat the people on top with appropriate deference.
3. Don't take words at face value. Read people's body language and expressions.

中华人民共和国外国人居留许可
RESIDENCE PERMIT FOR FOREIGNER IN THE PEOPLE'S REPUBLIC OF CHINA

名
Name ERICKSON SOPHIA CAMILLE

日期
Date 10 MAY 1993

护照号码
Passport No. 52619

日期
Date 14 MAR 2016

有效期至
Valid Until 01 M

地
at 河北廊坊

居留事由
Purpose of Residenc

注 无

CHAPTER THREE

Chinese Work Permits

�֎

The process of obtaining a Chinese work permit could best be described as a "bureaucratic nightmare." Navigating China's opaque legal system is a frustrating endeavor, but the patient and persevering are rewarded at the end with a degree of legitimacy that validates their efforts.

WORKING ILLEGALLY IN CHINA

Both expats and Chinese employers get frustrated with the complexity of the visa process, and it is not unusual to meet foreigners who are working without the correct visa or employment permit. Nor is it unusual for a Chinese company to turn a blind eye to your visa status when they hire you.

Quiz time: Is it advisable to work in China illegally?

(Hint: It's illegal)

Answer: No, it is not advisable to work in China without proper legal authorization. There are two potential risks to you:

1. Once you are in China you are at the mercy of your employer. You will not be able to appeal to the law if they cheat your or mistreat you in any way. Did your company promise you 18,000 RMB/month salary but they paid only 15,000 RMB? Tough luck. The worst case scenario is your company lies to you about the terms of your employment (forcing you to work overtime, paying less than you were promised), and when you quit they withhold your salary so that you are not able to pay for your plane ticket home. This situation is common enough that the U.S. Embassy in Beijing website clearly states that they will not fund your ticket home in this scenario.

2. The police occasionally run inspections in language schools, and if you are caught working illegally both you and your employer will suffer the consequences. Your employer will have to pay between 10,000 to 100,000 RMB fine and relinquish all its illegally earned income. The law is murkier on the fate of the illegal employee — the punishment should be based on the "severity of the case," aka the whim of the police officer arresting you. There are no criteria that objectively determine what makes one case more severe than the other, so you could be looking either at a fine between 5,000 and 20,000 RMB, immediate deportation, permanent visa blacklist in China, or 5-15 days in jail, or all of the above!

CAUTIONARY TALE

A kindergarten hired a Dutch girl to be an English teacher. Because of her nationality she could not get a teaching visa, but the company told her not to worry: They had paid off the police years ago not to look too closely at the foreign staff's visas.

After about a year the police stopped by for an inspection. This time the police head was unwilling to accept a bribe in exchange for silence. She and three other illegal employees were arrested and brought to a detention center. They were told they would be detained for 15 days and have to pay a heavy fine in order to be released (they were lucky that their employer agreed to pay the fine on their behalf).

For fifteen days she was held in what was essentially a jail cell with a dozen Chinese women. They were not allowed to speak to each other. During the day they were forced to sit together in an empty room, and if anyone moved or spoke a loud buzzer would go off until they stopped. The bedsheets were stained with congealed menstruation blood and feces. Thankfully the guards were not aggressive or

(continued)

violent, but it was a jarring experience for a sheltered Westerner.

After two weeks she was released, eight pounds lighter than when she started the ordeal. Tales like this are not common, but it does happen, and it is a risk to consider before engaging in illegal work.

Despite these risks, many expats continue to work illegally in China. For the most part nothing happens to them, but if you do meet the (rather lax) requirements for obtaining a work permit, why not just play it safe?

Many employers ask teachers to come to China on a tourist visa and switch afterwards. This is not advisable either because then you have no guarantee that your company is legally allowed to employ foreigners, and once you are in China it will be much more difficult for you to turn back if the work permit doesn't pan out. Demand your company provide all the material required for a Z visa before you buy your plane ticket to China.

HOW TO OBTAIN A CHINESE Z VISA

To work in China legally, you must enter under a Z Visa. There are two ways to obtain a Z visa.

1. Acquire a work permit
2. Acquire a Foreign Expert Certificate

Basic Requirements:

To be eligible for either of these documents, you need to meet the following criteria:

- Bachelor's degree
- Two years post-graduate experience
- Be between 24-60 years of age (24 is not set in stone, but to meet the bachelor's + two years experience most Americans will be this age)
- In good health (you will need to pass a medical examination)

How strict is the two years work experience requirement?

The biggest barrier young expats face in obtaining a Chinese work permit is the two years postgraduate work experience requirement. How strict are they about this?

In cities outside Beijing and Shanghai, the visa requirements are more relaxed. In Tier 2 or Tier 3 cities, you do not need work experience to be hired as a teacher.

In Beijing, you do need two years experience to apply for a work permit.

HOWEVER

Many ESL teachers work in China under a Foreign Expert Certificate instead of a work permit (both are legal). The requirements to obtain a Foreign Expert Certificate are a bachelor's degree, plus either two years postgraduate work experience or a TEFL/CELTA/equivalent certification demonstrating that you have passed a course on teaching English as a foreign language.

So if you do not have two years work experience, you will not be able to obtain a work permit, but you can work under a Foreign Expert Certificate if you complete a TEFL course.

HOW TO ACQUIRE A CHINESE WORK PERMIT

To basic process for obtaining a Chinese employment license is the following.

- Your employer provides you with an Employment License and a Letter of Invitation.
- You apply at your local Chinese embassy or consulate for a Z visa.
- You go to China.
- As soon as you arrive in China, your employer takes you to apply for a work permit and a residence permit at the police station.
  Step-by-step guide

Documents you must provide to apply for work visa

- An original copy of your bachelor's degree (they are very strict on this—photocopy is not acceptable, nor academic transcript)

- A health certificate
- If you have it, a TEFL/TESOL/CELTA certificate (these demonstrate that you passed a course on teaching English as a foreign language)
- A photocopy of your passport, which must have at least 6 months validity left
- A criminal background check (they are not very strict with this one—go to your local police station and ask them to provide a notarized document stating that you do not have a local criminal record)
- Your contract signature page

Before leaving for China

Step 1: Send a scanned copy of all the above documents to your employer. They will begin the process of obtaining a work permit invitation letter. It will take them two to four weeks to receive the necessary paperwork. While they are taking care of that, you can continue on to the following steps.

Step 2: Download and complete a visa application form for the Z visa (can easily be found online).

Step 3: Download a medical check form. Go to your local doctor and ask him or her to sign it. You will need to provide a passport size photo with the form. Then scan it and send it to your employer.

Step 4: Your employer will send you the work permit invitation letter via international courier (FedEx, DHL, etc.).

At this point, you should have the following documents in your possession:

- Work permit and invitation letter
- Z-class visa application form
- Signed and stamped medical certificate
- Passport
- 2" x 2" passport photo
- Visa fee of $150-200 depending on your nationality. Keep the receipts—employers will usually reimburse the cost once you arrive in China

Step 5: Go to the nearest Chinese embassy or consulate and apply for your Z visa. You should receive your visa within 3-5 working days.

After you arrive in China

Getting the Z visa is the most complicated part for you. Once you are in China your employer will help you take care of the rest of the process.

The Z visa does not permit you to work in China, it simply allows you to apply for a work permit once you are in the country. After you arrive, you will have 30 days to obtain the follow-up documentations: work permit and residence permit.

To apply for the work permit and residence permit, your employer will take you to get another health check in Beijing. You will also be taken to the local police station to register. Within a few weeks, you will be legally allowed to begin teaching. Congratulations!

HOW TO OBTAIN A FOREIGN EXPERTS CERTIFICATE

The alternative to obtaining a work permit is to work under a Foreign Experts Certificate. As of 2017, this is something you can do online as long as you meet the requirement of having majored in education or hold a TEFL certificate. Head to en.safea.gov.cn and click on Host Institution Registration. Submit your credentials, wait for it to be approved, then go to Foreign Expert Work Permit Application and Foreign Expert Certificate Application. You'll have to submit all the required documents to the appropriate authorities once you have been approved.

This is not an armed robber getting ready for a bank heist, but a woman wearing a "facekini" to protect the skin from the ravages of the sun.

CHINESE BEAUTY STANDARDS

Chinese people are not shy about remarking on each other's physical appearance. If you have skin problems, colleagues will offer you advice on how to fix it (don't eat spicy food). If you carry a few extra pounds, strangers will suggest you lose weight. If you have a prominent nose, Chinese girls will sigh and say they wish they had a big nose like yours.

As far as the Chinese are concerned, the whiter and thinner a woman, the more beautiful she is. There does not seem to be a lower end limit to this, and any girl who does not look downright emaciated will bemoan how fat she is. When I learned the words for "I need to lose weight" in Mandarin I suddenly understood half the conversations of my Chinese colleagues.

Skin whitening products are popular in beauty shops across Asia, as Chinese girls pursue that ghostly aesthetic. The slightest caress of a sunray will cause panic as women wield their parasols

CHINESE COMPLIMENTS

One compliment Westerners often receive in China is that our faces are very "three-dimensional." Chinese people dislike having flat faces, and admire Westerners for their prominent noses and facial planes.

This was a rude shock to my mother, who has always been sensitive about the size of her nose, when Chinese women tried to befriend her by saying, "I like your nose, it is so BIG!"

against the ravages of melanin production. A desire to protect the whiteness of the skin when no parasol is at hand has given rise to the "facekini."

Baifumei Or Gaofushuai?

The ideal girl in China is a Bai Fu Mei (white, rich, and beautiful). The ideal male is a Gao Fu Shuai (tall, rich, and handsome). For males generally the beauty standards are not as strict. As long as you are not fat and have no gross deformities you will escape criticism. But girls, either stay out of the sun and resist the McDonald's for a few months before moving to China, or grow a thick skin and a sense of humor about the vagaries of expectations placed on women across the world.

COFFEE CULTURE IN CHINA

After a few months in China I found myself thinking a blasphemous thought: "Coffee isn't good. I should quit drinking it." Afterwards I went back to the West for holiday and realized that the problem was not coffee, it was China. Coffee in China is expensive and unappetizing. Either so bland and weak it tastes like coffee-tea, or so bitter the flavor must be drowned in milk and sugar.

Despite this, cafe culture is starting to take root in the Middle Kingdom. Cafes are trendy with the millennials of Beijing and Shanghai, and businesses compete for their attention by outdoing each other in terms of niche decor. Cat cafes are all the rage these days, so expect to drink your latte with a fat Garfield lookalike snoring on your table. Beijing has an exact replica of the

> Standard price for a cup of coffee in a Beijing cafe: 25-30 RMB ($5-6)
>
> Don't forget to bring your French press!

cafe from "Friends" where the show plays on repeat and all the waiters take the names of a character. In Shanghai you'll find a toilet-inspired cafe, where they serve feces-shaped ice cream in urinal-shaped bowls.

One way in which cafes are not competing with each other is in terms of coffee quality, which remains abysmally low. You might get lucky and find one place that sells reliable brew, or you might decide to give up altogether and swap in your cappuccino for a cha-ppuccino (cha is tea in Mandarin, and the recent trend of cha-fes are a charming example of globalization with Chinese characteristics).

CHAPTER FOUR

The Great Firewall of China

E veryone's heard of the Great Wall of China, but its contemporary descendant, the Great Firewall, is less well-known. Both were built for essentially the same pur‐ pose—preventing barbaric Western hordes from destroying Chinese civilization.

There are some differences, however—the enemy today is Mark Zuckerberg, not Genghis Khan, and the fear of bar‐ baric nomadic tribesman has been supplanted by the threat of Facebook, Twitter, Instagram, and Snapchat.

Foreign websites are strictly restricted in China. Most of the popular social media platforms in the West have been blocked, and foreign news websites are getting banned one by one as they post articles the Chinese government deems untrue and seditious (i.e., anything that does more than uncritically praise the Communist Party and its steady helms‐ man Xi Jinping). As of 2016, here is a sampling of the websites that cannot be accessed via Mainland Chinese internet:

- Google and all associated pages (Gmail, Picasa, Google Maps, Google Docs, Google+, etc.)

- Facebook and Instagram

Attempts to police the morality of the Chinese internet has led to one of my favorite Chinese internet
regulations: It's forbidden for women to eat bananas
on streaming websites, as the censorship board determined that the act is too suggestive.

- YouTube
- Twitter
- The New York Times
- The Economist
- TIME
- Bloomberg
- BBC
- All porn websites

Before you panic at the idea of spending a year cut off from
the thrilling Facebook updates of your high school classmates
and incisive political commentary of distant relatives, realize there are ways to circumvent the Great Firewall. Virtual
Private Networks (VPNs) are ubiquitous in the phones and
computers of expats in China. VPNs allow you to send and
receive data from your device as if you are part of a separate
private or public network — if you are like me and have no idea

what that means, just understand that it allows your computer to pretend you are in D.C. (or London, or Amsterdam, or anywhere you want) while you are really in China.

It is highly recommended to download a VPN before you come to China, as many of the big providers are blocked in the mainland. Some are free, some cost money—as with most things, you get what you pay for. Free VPNs are notoriously unreliable, while the more expensive ones are usually dependable. A stable VPN costs around $50-100 and is a worthwhile investment.

VPNs aren't just useful because they allow you to post Sepia-filtered pictures of your trip to Yellow Mountain on Instagram. Even if you're not interested in following uncensored current events or keeping up with social media, VPNs will make your Chinese internet surfing experience much smoother. Foreign webpages load extremely slowly in China, as most pages come with buttons that are blocked (for example, a "share this on Facebook" option) which slow down the loading process. Unless you have the patience of a saint or are content to spend your time abroad exploring the Chinese cybersphere, you should install a reliable VPN on your phone and computer.

There are hundreds of different VPN providers. Here are some of the best options for China:

- **Astrill:** the most popular choice among expats. A bit on the pricey side at $70/year but generally well-regarded (www.astrill.com)

- **WiTopia:** one of the longest-running VPN servers in China. $40/year (www.witopia.net)
- **ExpressVPN:** very fast, very expensive. Best choice for the impatient among you, or Netflix aficionadas. $99.84/year (www.expressvpn.com)
- **StrongVPN:** my personal choice, not as well-known as the others but generally reliable. $69.96/year (www.strongvpn.com)
- **TunnelBear:** the great advantage of TunnelBear is that it is free. This means it is slower and less reliable than the paying options, but better than nothing. A good option for the miserly. $0/year (www.tunnelbear.com)

Stars burn brightly then collapse; empires rise to glory then crumble; VPNs load funny YouTube videos and then get banned. The catalogue of best VPNs to use in China is constantly evolving as the Great Firewall adapts to them, but the ones listed above have been reliable over the past half-decade. During particularly sensitive times (for example during the National People's Congress session in 2015), there will be a strict crackdown on VPNs and even the best connections will become unstable, but this is temporary and eventually normal service will resume.

A note on smartphones:

As mentioned above, Google and all affiliated pages are blocked in China. Android belongs to Google, which means that most Android apps don't work in China. So if you use an Android phone it is vital to download a VPN before you go so you can keep using your apps.

The iPhone is the best phone to bring to China as Apple is very popular there. If you use an iPhone, most of your apps will continue to work as long as they are not specifically banned by the censorship board. Additionally, iPhones are a status symbol in China and anyone who can afford one owns one, so your Apple logo will help you fit right in! (Just kidding, you will never fit in in China!)

Another option is to buy a phone once you arrive in China. This will ensure the apps you download work, but it also means you will be unable to install Google PlayStore unless you go through a very complicated process to circumvent the Firewall. There are some cheap, high-quality smartphone options in China—notably Huawei and Xiaomi—which will serve you well in the mainland, but will be difficult to bring home as they are set up to be incompatible with Android. It is possible to overcome this setting, but it takes IT skills and patience, which not all of us possess.

Other apps you must download before you come:

- **Baidu Maps:** This is essentially the same thing as Google Maps, with the key difference that it works in China. A little tricky to navigate at first as it is entirely in Mandarin, but the layout is the same as Google Maps so it is fairly easy to guess what you need to click to make it work. It's particularly useful if you speak no Chinese because it will save you having to ask locals for directions and then, if by some miracle they understand you, trying hopelessly to understand their answer. With Baidu Maps you can simply enter the address you're looking for and it will point arrows in the right direction for you. Once your character-reading ability progresses beyond illiteracy, you can use it to find recommended restaurants, bars, cafes, KTVs, and other attractions around you.

- **Pleco:** You will be deeply grateful to have this app when you have spicy tummy (la duzi, Chinese for diarrhea) and are desperately trying to find the nearest bathroom but realize you don't know how to say bathroom in Mandarin. Or in a shop and trying to figure out which of the bottles in front of you is laundry detergent and which is bleach. Or in a restaurant, trying to order something that is not fried pig innards or chicken feet. Pleco is the app everyone uses for Chinese-English translations, and can commonly be spotted in shops where foreigners point at it to ask for help in finding products. Its dictionary and translation services are free, and for a minor monthly fee you can add an option of having the app scan characters and translate them automatically, which can be very useful while reading menus or cheating on your Chinese homework.

- **WeChat:** This app is the best counterargument to anyone who says Western tech companies are more advanced than their Chinese counterparts. WeChat is a sort of hybrid of WhatsApp and Facebook, except far superior. You can use it to pay utilities, order a taxi, order takeout, buy plane and train tickets, find your true love, pay in shops, get promotional discounts, send your friends money, receive your friends' money, and sometimes receive free money from companies trying to advertise their products. Everyone in China uses WeChat for everything, and one of the most common requests you will receive after meeting someone is "Can I add your WeChat?" You will have to use this app in China, and you will learn to love it, and when you leave your biggest regret will be having to regress to primitive Western messaging apps. As they say, once you go WeChat you can never go back.

If you have all three of these apps installed before you get on the plane you are ahead of the game. Once you progress further in your China journey, you will also have to set up your AliPay and WeChat Wallet. But in order to that you need to have a Chinese bank account, so more on that later.

Perfect place to make new friends.

CHINESE TOILETS

Westerners are not graceful squatters. My students would some-times ask me to squat and then laugh delightedly as I clumsily fell on my bottom. We like to sit down on the floor, chair, or ideally a couch. Yet Chinese have been trained in the art of the squat since they learned to stand on their two feet. In the Beijing summer, street corners are filled with idlers perched on the balls of their feet, cigarette hanging from their mouths as they watch the world go by. Squatting is a useful art to master—it is a key skill you'll need in China, where most public bathrooms will require you to squat over a hole in the floor to do your business.

It's a difficult balancing act in the beginning as you clutch at the walls on either side of you, terrified of falling down a pipeline that looks like it has not been cleaned since it was first built thirty years ago. On the bright side, there is some evidence that squat toilets reduce hemorrhoids and constipation, so think of these long-term benefits next time you tip over and fall into bathroom floor mystery sludge.

Even more difficult than adjusting to squat toilets is adjusting to open toilets. These are common in the hutong areas of Beijing and outside large cities. The restroom will be a large open space with 6-8 toilets either side by side or in a circle. They can be a sociable place during "flush hour" in the morning or bedtime—hutong houses rarely have private bathrooms so these public toilets serve entire neighborhoods. Women squat around chatting with each other and watching TV shows on their phones while their men squat next door smoking and playing video games. If you're searching for a place to meet real locals, look no further. They will be unabashedly chatty as you partake in this universal human ritual together.

And make sure to bring your own toilet paper when you use any restroom away from home. Very few Chinese restrooms have paper, even in restaurants, bars, shops, and the like. You know you're at a chic establishment if they provide customers with toilet paper. You'll quickly learn to carry around a pack of Kleenex at all times. As for soap, forget about it. Most public bathrooms don't even have a sink. If you see a bathroom with soap you're probably at the Ritz-Carlton.

CHAPTER FIVE

Fresh off the Boeing

⁂

You took the plunge. You survived the fourteen hours of flight, you're exhausted, smelly, and dishevelled. You have your first encounter with the Chinese mob as you wait two hours in the swarming mass of locals and foreigners fighting to pass through immigration. You wait tensely, sure that the impassive gatekeepers of China are just waiting for the opportunity to throw a criminal like you in jail for coming in on the wrong visa. You breathe a sigh of relief when yours stamps your passport with barely a bored glance in your direction.

You always wondered what kind of VIP jet-setters had drivers with a name placard waiting for them in the arrival gates, and now you're one of them. A young Chinese woman comes forward to greet you. You extend your hand and she allows you to squeeze her limp fingers with the typical Chinese tolerance of weird foreigner customs. You will soon give up the habit of extending your hand to strangers.

Welcome to China!

At first glance it doesn't look radically different from a Western city: modern buildings, wide boulevards, streets clogged with traffic. Then you notice subtle differences:

mopeds laden with water barrels and fruit whizzing on the sidewalk. Half the women are hiding under umbrellas despite the fact it is 95 degrees and sunny. Dozens of old women on a square are dancing in unison to loud pop music.

Welcome to Beijing!

The following chapter will explain how to set up your life to be as smooth as possible while you're here:

HOW TO GET A PHONE

The first order of business will be buying a sim card, because in order to do anything else (open bank account, rent house, etc.) you will need a Chinese phone number. A Chinese sim card can be inserted into a foreign phone, or you can buy a new Chinese phone.

Chinese tech companies used to be considered very cheap and very low quality, but they have experienced a resurgence in recent years and there are now many excellent phone brands. There are rumors that they come with spyware for government surveillance preinstalled, but unless you are planning to use your Huawei to plan a coup against the Communist Party you probably don't need to worry about this. Here are the biggest Chinese phone companies:

Chinese Phone Brands

- **Xiaomi:** Basically a shameless copy of the iPhone, but at half the price.

You are lucky to have an author with vast personal experience with Chinese phone brands, having gone through six phones during her time in Beijing.

The cursed fates of Sophia's phones:

1. Coolpad, pickpocketed in Vietnam
2. Huawei I, dropped on the floor of a nightclub
3. Xiaomi, fell off a boat in Malaysia
4. Huawei II, gone MIA under circumstances mysterious to this day
5. Vivo, left in the seat of a taxi
6. Meizu, still faithfully by my side today, which is ironic since I only bought it because it was the cheapest phone in the store, figuring I would lose it soon anyway, and so far it is my longest-lasting phone ever (yes I am annoyed about this)

- **Huawei:** Huawei's high-end phones are world-class. Mate 10 takes fantastic photos, has long-lasting battery life, useful features like counts your steps and calories burned

  Cheap Huawei phones are awful. Very short battery life, bad pictures, slow loading, break easily

- **Vivo:** If you're looking for a good, cheap phone, this is it

- **Coolpad:** The original Chinese phone: cheap and low-quality

How to Buy a Chinese Sim Card

There are three major mobile carriers in China: China Mobile (中国移动), China Unicom (中国联通), and China Telecom (中国电信).

China Telecom is seldom used by foreigners since for the most part it is only compatible with Chinese phones when it comes to 2G, 3G, and 4G.

China Mobile is the most popular — their shops are ubiquitous across Beijing, and once you have your sim card you will be able to go there to top up your phone whenever you need (you can also do this through text). However, China Mobile 3G is incompatible with many foreign phones, so unless you want to use 2G or 4G you will need a Chinese phone. China Unicorn is compatible with most foreign phones on 2G, 3G and 4G. Both China Mobile and China Unicorn have excellent coverage and modest fees so either is a viable option.

However, in order to initially buy a sim card, foreigners are required to present their passports. This cannot be done at any mobile shops, as most of them can only register sim cards with a national ID card (which only Chinese citizens possess). Some shops are not equipped to give sim cards to foreigners, in which case you should ask them to point you in the direction of a store that can help you set up your account.

Go to the store and tell the shopkeeper you want to buy a sim card (in Chinese it's pronounced simka). He probably will not speak English but he will be able to understand your request.

LUCKY PHONE NUMBERS

Once you select a plan, the shopkeeper will give you a stack of cards or show you a screen with all the different phone numbers available. Some will cost 50 RMB, others up to 500 RMB.

This can be confusing to foreigners who don't understand the price discrepancy. Essentially it's a superstition thing—Chinese people believe certain numbers are good or bad (for example, four sounds like death in Mandarin so it's unlucky, while eight sounds like fortune and is therefore lucky), and they will try to pick an auspicious phone number. If you don't care about this, just buy the cheapest option.

You'll notice in China that people are always buried nose deep in their phone, especially on subway or public transportation. This is because data is very cheap. The basic plan costs approximately 66 RMB (less than $10), and gives you 50 minutes of calling, 240 SMS, and 300MB of 3G data. There are other options if you need more data or calling time. The shopkeeper will give you a pamphlet explaining the various deals available.

Once you have chosen the phone number, the shop attendant will photocopy your passport and set up your sim card.
You can now top it up by however much you want.

Top It Up Online

You can easily pay your phone bill online through WeChat
Wallet, which I will explain how to set up in just a moment.
Go to your WeChat Wallet → Mobile Top-Up → enter your
phone number, and you're done! You can also ask a friend
to do it with their WeChat Wallet if you don't have yours set
up; they simply need to enter your phone number and the
amount you want to pay.

Now that you have a phone number, you can set up your
bank account.

HOW TO SET UP A BANK ACCOUNT

Usually your employer will tell you which bank they use
to pay their salary, and they will help you open an account
with them. If they don't, here are the biggest banks in China:

- ABC (Agricultural Bank of China)
- Bank of China
- Bank of Communication
- China Construction Bank
- China Merchants Bank
- ICBC (Industrial and Commercial Bank of China)

THE ROSETTA STONE: CHINGLISH EDITION

In China, family name comes first, followed by given name.

So Jackie Chan → Chan Jackie (陈港生)
Tanyi Wang → Wang Tanyi

In official documents, Western names are often translated this way.

Sophia Erickson → ERICKSONSOPHIA

For foreigners it doesn't make a real difference which bank you choose, so pick based on convenience. Which bank has the most number of branches and ATMs in your neighborhood? Keep in mind that if you need to get a new card, change your pin, report an issue, etc., you cannot just go to any branch of your bank, you have to go to the one where you opened your account. So it's important to pick a branch you can easily access.

What documents will you need?

Opening a bank account is a surprisingly simple procedure in China. All you need is your passport, phone number, and

CAUTIONARY TALE

Always check if your travel destination accepts UnionPay cards. Don't make the same mistake I did and end up trapped on a small Malaysian island with no money to buy your ferry ticket back because they don't accept Chinese cards on the island's lone ATM.

a 10-30 RMB deposit. Some banks might charge you another 20 RMB to pay for your card, so take about 50 RMB with you just to be safe.

When you get to the bank, go to the information desk. If you don't speak Chinese, bring a Mandarin note explaining that you want to open a bank account (我想开银行账户 Wǒ xiǎng kāi yínháng zhànghù). You will have to fill out a form, which will often have English translations. If the form is entirely in Chinese, the service person will help you fill out the information. They will then give you a number and ask you to wait in the lobby. Once your number is called, simply present yourself at the counter and hand over your form and passport. At one point you will be asked to create a PIN code (these are 6 digits long in China), and then you can leave with your bank card in hand.

UnionPay

Chinese bank cards use a UnionPay chip. UnionPay cards can be used in ATMs across Asia and are becoming commonly accepted in Western countries as Chinese tourists steadily continue to take over the world. But if you're going to a remote area, play it safe and bring plenty of cash with you because UnionPay is still not as internationally accepted as Visa and Mastercard.

How to set up your AliPay and WeChat Wallet

With your phone and bank card in hand, you are now able to set up your WeChat Wallet and AliPay. China is fast on the way to becoming a cashless society, and cards are being phased out in favor of these fast and convenient payment apps. Many little hole-in-the-wall shops that do not accept cards will take payments through these apps, and I've even stumbled on a few places that won't accept cash either.

Wechat Wallet

Go to the "Me" tab of your Wechat account. The third button down will say "Wallet."

Click on the "Cards" button. From there it will ask if you want to link your bank card. You will need to provide your card number, phone number, and name (exactly as it appears on your bank account, so make sure to keep your account

TAOBAO-CCO:
CHINA'S ADDICTION EPIDEMIC

Taobao is the world's largest online retailer. It is a massive unregulated bazaar whose goods and services range from baby foxes to a pretend boyfriend to bring home to your family over the holiday (a surprisingly popular service for young Chinese facing intense pressure to get married).

Shopping on Taobao is like playing Russian roulette—sometimes you end up with an extraordinarily cheap, high-quality find, other times you try to order shoes and find the seller has sent you only one, and when you complain he will tell you shoes must be bought individually.

Warning: Taobao is highly addictive. Shopping on Taobao may have severe repercussions on your bank account.

information. Because this is China your bank might have registered your name in a counter-intuitive way, so John Michael Smith could be written as SMITHJOHNMICHAEL).

You will receive an SMS with a verification code. Once you enter the code your bank account and WeChat will be linked, and you can transfer money from your bank card into your Wallet. From then on you can start using your WeChat Wallet to pay your phone bill, utilities, taxis, and send your friends money.

AliPay: AliPay is owned by Tencent Holdings, Ltd., one of the largest internet companies in the world. AliPay and WeChat Wallet provide similar services in terms of cashless payment, but AliPay also allows you to shop on Taobao.

Until recently, foreigners could not set up an AliPay account since it required a Chinese national ID card, but it is now possible to open an account with a passport as long as you use one of the following banks:

Bank of China, China Citic Bank, China Guangfa Bank (CGB), China Merchant's Bank, China Minsheng Bank, Everbright Bank, Hangzhou Bank, Industrial Bank, Industrial & Commercial Bank of China (ICBC), Pingan Bank, Postal Savings Bank of China (PSBC) and Shanghai Pudong Development Bank (SPD)

AliPay app can be used in English, so it is very straight-forward to link your bank card. Again, you'll need a Chinese bank card, phone number, and your name exactly as it appears on your bank account. You will have to create a four-digit PIN code to use on the app.

If you succeed, you will be able to transfer money from your bank account onto AliPay, and a whole new world of online shopping will open to your fingertips!

How to Use AliPay and WeChat Wallet

If you want to use these apps in a restaurant or shop, ask the service person for either:

- Alipay is called zhifubao: jour (as in journal)-foo-bow (支付宝)
- WeChat Wallet is weixinbao: way-sheen-bow (微信宝)

CHINESE NAMES

Chinese parents don't typically name their children after people (so no Adams, Marys, Josephs, etc.), and prefer to invent original names for each generation.

These names are beautiful when translated — Love Country, Clear as Jade, Spring Plum — yet students usually choose to pick their own names in English.

The result is often amusing, and a favorite pastime of ESL teachers is comparing the English names of their students.

Some of my personal favorites from my two years of teaching: Watermelon, Summer Rain, Wolf Hunter, God, and Pussy Cat (had a tough time explaining to that girl why she should change her name before going to America).

SCAM WARNING

The most common trick is for people to walk around the subway and ask you to scan their code to support their new online shopping business, although you'll sometimes see fake advertisements on the wall with treacherous QR codes. Don't go around scanning codes willy-nilly, only scan reputable companies or shops you are buying from.

They will likely point out a QR code for you to scan. QR codes look like this:

Once you've scanned the code, you will be asked to enter an RMB amount and then you can send money.

A Note on QR Codes

QR codes never really took off in the United States but they are ubiquitous in China. If you want to add someone on WeChat you will scan a QR code, if you want to follow a company you will scan a QR code, if you want to receive a discount you might be asked to scan a QR code. For the most part these QR codes are a fast and convenient way to get connected on social media, but there are some cases when scanning a QR code will give your phone a virus, or worse, give someone access to your AliPay and WeChat Wallet money.

With your phone, bank account, and AliPay you are now ready to become a movie-watching, online-shopping, utilities-paying integrated member of the Chinese economy. Congratulations, you are no longer a FOB (Fresh off the Boeing)!

THE TEN COMMANDMENTS
OF THE LAOWAI BIBLE

For many Chinese, their English teacher is the only foreigner they will ever personally interact with. This means if their English teacher is a drunk, foul-mouthed and oversexed American, they will believe that all Americans are drunk, foul-mouthed and oversexed.

In order to promote world peace and goodwill, here are some guidelines you should follow during your time in China:

1. Thou shalt not kill
2. Thou shalt not commit adultery
3. Thou shalt not steal
4. Thou shalt not bear false witness against thy neighbor
5. Thou shalt not covet
6. Thou shalt drink as much as thou liketh, but thou shalt not get belligerent and thou shalt limit thy public puking. Thou shalt try not to look like an idiot.

7. Gentlemen: Thou shalt not take pride in taking advantage of Chinese maidens. In fact, thou shalt not take advantage of Chinese maidens at all and thou shalt avoid sleeping with them if that is the extent to which thou intendest to acknowledge their existence (this also applies to laowai maidens, but is less of an issue due to the universal gender double standard when it comes to sleeping around)

8. Thou shalt not deface national monuments. There is no need to carve thine initials into the Great Wall, if thou wanteth proof that thou hast been, thou shalt take a selfie

9. Thou might think thou art a gentle shepherd guiding thine students towards truth when thou tellest them about Western interpretations of Chinese history, but all thou art accomplishing is making them feel attacked and resentful and eager to point out the flaws and hypocrisies of the West.

10. Thou shalt be respectful of Chinese culture. Obviously that means thou shalt not say that spitting is gross, TCM is stupid, and Chinese people are ugly. It also means that when thou talkest about China, thou shalt praise much and criticize little. Americans don't like to hear that we are fat and ignorant and our government has caused untold destruction across the world. Neither do the Chinese.

Not all Americans are "open"; not all Chinese are traditional. Some Chinese love drinking and casual sex. Some hate their government and are eager for a willing conversant with whom to share their opprobrium. But until you understand who you are dealing with, follow these Ten Commandments to avoid causing offense.

HOW TO DEAL WITH CULTURE SHOCK

Culture shock is an inevitable part of changing countries, particularly when going between continents with such vast cultural differences as East and West. Culture shock generally manifests itself as feelings of depression, homesickness, criticism for everything in the new culture, and contempt for the local people.

Culture shock usually takes a few weeks to strike. First comes the honeymoon period, when everything is new and exciting: you celebrate every difference you encounter in the new culture, eager for good pictures and stories to share with your friends back home. The restaurants only have chopsticks, how fun! Men are smoking indoors, how quaint! I have to use a squat toilet, how amusing! Eventually this turns into: the restaurants only have chopsticks, can't I eat a single meal without spilling food all over myself? Men are smoking indoors, are they trying to give me lung cancer? I have to use a squat toilet, am I some kind of animal? You get infuriated by trivial things, like the fact your waiter was unfriendly, and blow small incidents out of proportion until they become a scathing indictment of the new culture as a whole.

You might be the most open-minded, adventurous, China-enamored laowai to ever grace God's green earth, but unless you have renounced all earthly suffering and attained nirvana, you will deal with some of the feelings listed above. It's alienating to move to a country where you can't understand anyone, you can't read, the food is wildly different (and probably makes you sick), you feel like a child who needs help going to the supermarket to do his shopping, and you have difficulty understanding social cues which you never once had to think about in your life until now.

Strategies for dealing with culture shock include:

1. Recognize that you are experiencing culture shock. It helps if you are aware of the symptoms and realize that your feelings don't necessarily mean that you have made a terrible mistake, but that you are going through a perfectly normal transition period.

2. Meet and befriend people of the local culture. It is harder to tell yourself, "Ugh, Chinese people are rude and stupid!" when you have many Chinese friends who are neither rude nor stupid. (Harder but not impossible. Many racists successfully maintain friendships across racial lines, performing impressive feats of mental acrobatics to justify these conflicting attitudes. Don't be one of them). So make an effort to join classes, events, and activities where you will meet Chinese people with similar interests to yours.

3. Stop yourself from getting into a cycle of negativity. This means don't indulge in endless complaining about China with other bitter expats. Look for the positives, recognize that every culture has good points and weak points and going through life looking for reasons to criticize is a recipe for unhappiness.

4. Give it time. At the height of your culture shock you might think there is no way you could ever learn to tolerate your new environment, let alone like it, but if you force yourself to stay open-minded and make an effort to integrate, these

feelings will pass. Most expats I know said it took about three months before they started to adjust to and enjoy their time in China.

The good news is that culture shock is not fatal. It's like the mental version of the stomach bug most people get when moving to China: You will question your decision to move in the beginning when every meal seems to be followed by an emergency trip to the bathroom, but once you get over it you will wonder how you managed to live so long without tasting the wonder of mala and jianbing. Don't be one of those laowai who eats every meal at McDonald's because they ate a pancake that made them sick once so they gave up on Chinese food forever.

Once you have surmounted culture shock, you can look forward to eventually dealing with its counterpart: reverse culture shock, when you go home and realize it's not as great as you remember.

I will let you figure that one out by yourself. Good luck!

明

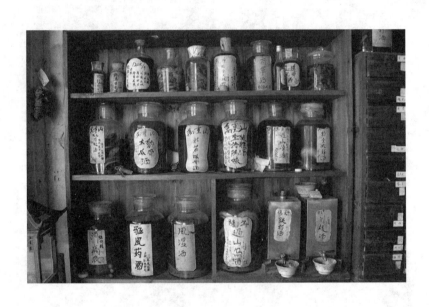

CHAPTER SIX

Healthcare in China

HEALTH INSURANCE

Even if you are young and invincible, you should buy health insurance before moving to China. Accidents happen—scooters collide, hikers fall off cliffs, drunks get into bar fights—and if you are not covered and don't have enough cash to pay for treatment out of pocket, chances are you will be turned away at the door. This is true of most Chinese hospitals even if the situation is life or death.

Chinese citizens usually get health coverage from their place of employment. Some work places will offer health insurance for foreigners as well, though this is not guaranteed. Make sure you to ask. If you are not covered, you should buy your own health coverage.

How to Pick a Health Insurance

This guide is geared to recent graduates who are enjoying the health and vigor of youth. Healthy young people can most likely get away with a budget health insurance package that covers emergencies and hospitalization. This will give you security so that you are not completely screwed if

> **EXTREMELY IMPORTANT:** If you get into a car
> accident and are in a life and death situation, need-
> ing immediate intensive care, and you do not have
> insurance and cannot pay the cost in cash up front,
> you will be turned away at the door of a Chinese
> hospital.

you get in a car crash, but it will not cover serious illnesses,
long-term conditions, cancer, etc.

Health coverage of this kind can cost as low as 3,500 RMB
a year. Some expats have the attitude that since health care
in China is cheap anyway (a couple thousand RMB at most
for several days in the hospital) they prefer to pay out of
pocket if need be rather than spend the extra money each
year.

There are two problems with this approach:

(1) Without health insurance you will probably have
to go to a public Chinese hospital instead of an international clinic, where costs can be prohibitive. Public Chinese
hospitals are generally fine but not up to standards that
Westerners are used to. Long waits, lack of privacy, no
English-speakers, and questionable hygiene make visits to
public hospitals unpleasant for expats.

(2) Most importantly, if you get into an accident and
need surgery, or transportation to a hospital that can

SCAM ALERT

Chinese doctors are public servants. As such they are not paid a high salary.

However, they do make money off selling medicine. The result is that doctors will push you to buy unnecessary medicine in order to generate income. This is a common scam in public hospitals.

Educate yourself about your illness and check online for the kind of medicine you should be buying. Do some research on your doctor's prescription.

The active ingredients of the medicine should be written in English on the box.

provide adequate care, you might not have the necessary 10,000 RMB in cash available, and this could literally mean death. Is that a risk you are willing to take?

Points to Keep in Mind When Picking Health Insurance Plan

Why is it a bad idea to stay on travel insurance?

Travel insurance plans like Global Nomad are much cheaper than regular health insurance, and they will cover you abroad for only about $100 a year. The problem with keeping a travel insurance is that as soon as you establish residency in a country (in Beijing, this would mean full-time job, registered in an apartment, residency permit) you will be ineligible to file a claim with them in case of need. You will be able to use them while traveling, but not in China. So even though $100 is much cheaper than 3000 RMB, travel insurance will be useless to you once you are settled in China.

Direct Billing

Most private hospitals and some public hospitals in Beijing, Shanghai, and Guangzhou accept direct billing. But the majority of Chinese hospitals do not. This means if you go to a public hospital, you will have to pay out of pocket, then file a separate insurance claim later.

It is important to check out which local hospital accepts direct billing so that you can go there when you need it. Simply ask your insurer which Chinese hospitals they have a direct relationship with. Try to pick the insurance most convenient to you in this regard, with a nearby hospital that will accept direct billing.

Waiting Period

Many health insurers have a waiting period of up to several years before you can start using their services. That means you will have paid one or more years of fees, but you will still not be able to bill them for your medical expenses. Obviously, if you are picking one right before moving to China, you want a short waiting period.

Dental Work

Many health insurers provide a dental insurance plan for only a couple hundred dollars more. Yet dental care in China is extremely cheap (it should not exceed a couple hundred RMB per session), and you would most likely save money by paying out of pocket if necessary.

In case of extreme dental care (as in you get in an accident and half your teeth are knocked out), your medical insurance will usually cover the cost.

Personal Liability

You should consider getting personal liability insurance. This means, for example, if you cause someone else to break their bones and they ask you to pay for their medical costs, the insurance will pay for you. It could come in handy, though this is not a life-and-death situation like getting your own emergency health insurance.

Deductibles

You should choose a health insurance with low deductibles, as Chinese health care tends to be quite cheap in the first place. There's no point paying a $100 deductible if most Chinese health care does not exceed $75 . Try to get a plan with deductibles as close to 0 as possible.

Transportation And Repatriation

In case of serious life-threatening injury, a standard Chinese hospital might not be able to provide adequate treatment.

Medical evacuation back to your home country costs run as high as 50,000 RMB, so it's a good idea to get a plan that covers transportation and repatriation.

You might even look into an insurance plan that will take your remains home, but that is getting a little morbid.

International Health Insurance Plans:

Keeping all these points in mind, here is a list of the top health insurers for expats in China. Browse around their website and call them up to ask questions to find the one most suitable for you:

- AIGG Global Health: www.chartisinsurance.com.cn/en/en_index.html
- Allianz Worldwide Care: www.allianzworldwidecare.com
- Bupa International: www.bupainternational.com
- IMG ProtExPlan: www.protexplan.com
- MSH China (also GBG): www.mshchina.com
- Ping An: insurance.pingan.com
- William Rusell: www.william-russell.com
- CIGNA: www.cigna.com
- Aetna: www.aetna.com
- AXA TP: www.axapppinternational.com
- Now Health: www.now-health.com

HOSPITALS IN CHINA

Understand that Chinese people go to the hospital for any kind of illness—flu, pregnancy, or broken bones. China doesn't have a tradition of family doctor or general practitioners. Whatever ails them, they find the relevant department in the local hospital and talk directly to the doctors there.

There are two kinds of hospitals in China: public and international. As you can imagine, public hospitals are cheaper but quality of care is lower. International hospitals are more expensive, but quality of care is up to first world standards.

What to Expect from a Chinese Public Hospital:

1. Big crowds and long waiting times

2. Dubious hygiene conditions

3. Total lack of privacy. As a foreigner you will stand out, which will make the problem worse. Chinese people do not really understand the concept of privacy.

4. No English speakers

5. All forms must be filled out in Mandarin

6. Most likely no direct billing to international health insurers, so you might have to pay out of pocket, then file a claim separately with your insurance company

7. Cheap prices

8. Traditional Chinese Medicine will be taken seriously and offered as potential treatment

What to expect from an international hospital:

1. Doctors are either foreign or foreign-educated
2. Everyone speaks English
3. Privacy and individual care
4. Hygienic environment on par with Western standards
5. Speedy service
6. Prices up to 10x higher than public hospitals

List of Hospitals in Beijing

International Hospitals

International hospitals are much more expensive than public hospitals — price for a consultation is usually around 400-900 RMB, and treatment costs run into the several thousand RMB. International health insurance plans will cover this. Additionally, international hospitals typically offer services in English, French, Spanish, Korean, Japanese, and many other languages.

Beijing United Family and Clinics (BJU)
BJU was opened in Beijing in 1997. It offers a wide variety of services and has smaller clinics opened all around Beijing.

BJU is the only hospital in Beijing accredited by Joint Commission International (JCI) as offering medical care on par with the best hospitals in the United States and Europe. It is also by far the most expensive hospital in Beijing.

Address: 2 Jiangtai Lu Chaoyang District 朝阳区 将台路2号

Phone number: +86 10 5927 7000

Opening hours: Mon-Sat 8:30 A.M.-5:30 P.M. 24-hour emergency care

Website: beijing.ufh.com.cn

Beijing International SOS Clinic
Opened in 1989, International SOS offers a wide variety of services, diagnostics, fully stocked pharmacy, and 24/7 emergency care.

Address: China, Beijing Shi, Chaoyang Qu, 琨莎中心1座 Kunsha Center Parking Lot, 新源里16号 邮政编码: 100027

Phone number: +86 10 6462 9100

Opening hours: Every day 8 A.M.-8 P.M., 24-hour emergency care

Website: www.internationalsos.com/clinicsinchina/en/Beijing.aspx

International Medical Center Beijing
IMC offers services ranging from dermatology, OB/GYN, dental care, as well as traditional Chinese medicine and integrative medicine.

Address: S106, S111 Lufthansa Center, 50 Liangmahe Lu Chaoyang District 朝阳区 亮马桥路50号燕莎中心写字楼1层 S106

Phone number: +86 10 6462 2079

Opening hours: 24-hour emergency care; for other services it depends on the department. All are open at least 8 A.M. to 5:30 P.M. every day.

Website: www.imcclinics.com/english

Hong Kong International Medical Clinic
Offers services ranging from ophthalmology to dental care to X-rays. Has fully-stocked pharmacy for both Western medicine and traditional Chinese medicine. Price for a basic consultation is 680 RMB, with a follow-up fee of $30.

Address: 9/F, office tower of the Swissôtel, 2 Chaoyangmen Beidajie Dongcheng District 东城区 北京港澳国际医务诊所, 朝阳门北大街2号港澳中心瑞士酒店办公楼9层

Phone number: +86 10 6553 2288

Opening hours: Daily 9 A.M.-9 P.M. (nursing service available after 9pm)

Website: www.hkclinic.com

OASIS International Hospital
Opened in 2012, OASIS International is the most recent addition to Beijing's international hospitals. Offers full range of service — emergency care, dermatology, pediatrics,

mental health, ENT, traditional Chinese medicine, etc. State of the art technology, modern and well-furnished.

Address: 9 Jiuxianqiao Beilu Chaoyang District 朝阳区 酒仙桥北路9号

Phone number: 400-8762-747

Opening hours: Mon-Sat 8:30 A.M.-5:30 P.M. (some clinics open from 8:30 A.M.-12:30 P.M.), daily 24-hours emergency care

Website: www.oasishealth.cn

Bayley & Jackson Medical Center
Bayley & Jackson was originally a Hong Kong hospital that has expanded to open branches all over the world. Services provided include OB/GYN, pediatrics, health check-up, dental services, and TCM.

Address: 7 Ritan Donglu Chaoyang District 朝阳区 日坛东路7号

Phone number: +86 10 8562 9998

Opening hours: Mon-Sat 9 A.M.-6 P.M.

Website: www.bjhealthcare.com

Amcare Women's & Children's Hospital
Amcare is Beijing's leading hospital specializing in maternity, OB/GYN, and pediatric care for mid- to high-range price. They currently have two branches open in Beijing.

First branch

Address: Bldg 5 Anhui Beili Yiyuan Chaoyang District 朝阳区 朝阳区安慧北里逸园5号楼

Phone number: 400 100 0016

Opening hours: 24 hours daily

Second branch

Address: 9 Fangyuan Xilu Chaoyang District 朝阳区 芳园西路9号

Phone number: 6434 2399 24-hour hotline, 800 610 6200

Opening hours: 8 A.M.-4:30 P.M. daily

Website: www.amcare.com.cn

Public Hospitals

There are dozens of public hospitals spread around Beijing. The three listed here are the largest and have the best reputation for general care. All three of them also provide direct billing for a number of international health insurers.

Peking Union Medical College Hospital

PUMCH was founded in 1921 by the China Medical Board in NYC under the Rockefeller Foundation, and has since then maintained the reputation as the best public hospital in Beijing. It has much cheaper prices than the international clinics, but a longer waiting period. Registration cost is 100-300 RMB, and consultation with a doctor is 200 RMB or higher. It has a wing set aside for foreigners with

English-speaking staff (but be warned, prices in this wing are more expensive. As a foreigner you are not obligated to go the foreign wing, so if you want to save money, go to the regular registration). Offers services in OB/GYN, pediatrics, ENT, traditional Chinese medicine, ophthalmology, surgery, internal medicine, etc.

Address: 1 Shuaifuyuan, Wangfujing (the foreigners' wing is located behind and to the left of the main hospital entrance) Dongcheng District 东城区 王府井帅府园1号 （接待外国人的区域在主楼的左后方）

Phone number: +86 10 6915 6114

Opening hours: Mon-Fri 8 A.M.-5 P.M.

Website: www.pumch.cn/Index.html

Beijing Friendship Hospital
Beijing Friendship Hospital is affiliated with the Capital University of Medical Sciences, founded in 1952. Beijing Friendship Hospital offers direct billing with a number of international health insurers. Basic consultation costs 70 RMB, 100 RMB, or 200 RMB, dependent on expertise of doctor.

Address: 95 Yong'an Lu Xuanwu District 宣武区 永安路95号

Phone number: 010-63016616

Opening hours: Daily 6:30 A.M.-4:30 P.M., 24-hour emergency care

Website: www.bfh.com.cn

China-Japan Friendship Hospital

Given the hostile relationship between the Chinese and Japanese governments, China-Japan Friendship Hospital has an inauspicious name. Yet for a Chinese public hospital it enjoys a good reputation. Offers services in OB/GYN, emergency care, check-up, pediatrics, internal medicine, ENT and orthopedics. Basic consultation fee is 100 RMB. Has fully-stocked pharmacy offering Western and Chinese medicine. Also has a foreigner wing, though again, costs there are much higher — 500 RMB for registration, expensive treatments.

Address: Yinghua Donglu, Heping Jie Chaoyang District 朝阳区 和平街樱花东路

Phone number: +86 10 8420 5566

Opening hours: 24-hour emergency service

Website: english.zryhyy.com.cn

Michael Phelps bringing TCM to international attention during the 2016 Olympics. The round bruises come from the practice of "cupping"

TRADITIONAL CHINESE MEDICINE

One of the most enduring legacies of China's ancient history is its traditional medicine (TCM), which has as much influence today as it did one thousand years ago. It coexists side-by-side with Western medicine, both of which are seen as having a separate but equal role in society (well, maybe not equal—Chinese methods are always best).

Chinese eagerly seek international recognition of the value of TCM. When Tu Youyou won the 2015 Nobel Prize in Physiology or Medicine for her discovery of a treatment for malaria based on traditional cures, it was heralded as irrefutable proof of the superiority of Chinese medicine. When Michael Phelps and various athletes were pictured covered in "cupping" bruises during the

2016 Olympics, the Chinese media went wild at the international attention cast on this ancient practice.

Some TCM methods have indeed been found to be medically sound ways of treating ailments. Other claims are more dubious. Here is a list of common conceptions Chinese people hold based on ideas rooted in TCM:

- Cold liquids are bad for your health. Chinese rarely drink any cold beverages—even plain water is served boiling hot in restaurants. This is fine in the winter but frustrating in the summer when you need an iced drink to cool you off, and after much negotiation with the waiter, he brings you a handful of ice cubes and a pot of boiling tea.
- You should eat spicy food in the summer but not in the winter, otherwise the imbalance of temperature inside your stomach and outside will make you sick.
- After giving birth, women must lie in bed and avoid showering for one month. It is believed the reason white women age faster than Chinese women is because we do not follow this practice.

Any attempt to bring up scientific evidence refuting these claims will be met with the stock answer: "Yes, but Chinese bodies are different from everyone else." This is seen as an incontrovertible argument, and after hearing that you might as well give up because you will be arguing with a wall.

Interestingly, Chinese doctors do not enjoy the same respect in society as Western doctors. Because there is no official licensing

Traditional Chinese Medicine

THE ROSETTA STONE: QI-NGLISH EDITION

TCM is based on ancient ideas about life energy, or "qi" (pronounced "chee"), which must circulate evenly throughout the body in order for humans to remain healthy. When you fall sick, it means the qi has become clogged somewhere, and in order to be restored to health you will need to find a way to let the qi flow again. Acupuncture and massages can help release extraneous qi from your body so you will be back in balance. It bears vague resemblance to traditional Western medicinal view that illnesses were caused by imbalances of the various humors in the body (phlegm, bile, blood, etc.) which had to be restored to balance in order to maintain health.

process to become a TCM doctor, the industry is suffused with hacks and charlatans. Nevertheless, TCM holds a revered position in Chinese society and you will certainly encounter its influence during your time here.

A CURE FOR THE COMMON COLD?

One smoggy Beijing winter, I decided to step into a massage parlor I often walked by, advertising 30-minute sessions for 30 RMB.

I chatted with the masseuse for a while, who remarked that I had a cold. She then asked me a question I couldn't understand. I deployed my usual tactic in this situation: smile, nod, and hope for the best.

What followed were the most agonizing thirty minutes of my life, as she energetically rubbed and kneaded burning stones across my back. It was the first massage I'd ever had. I had heard that massages are supposed to be painful but I couldn't believe people willingly subjected themselves to this. I gritted my teeth and stuck it through to the end, vowing to never step into a massage parlor again.

A friend was with me at the time, and when it was over she said in a voice that was obviously trying to hide her concern. "Uh, your back is pretty red. Are you okay?" She took a picture and showed me. My back was crisscrossed with purple and scarlet welts. I looked like a slave who had been whipped for trying to escape the plantation. I sent a picture to my parents, who told me I must have stumbled upon a masseuse who hates Americans and jumped on the opportunity to torture one, and I should call the police on her.

The next day at work, I told my colleague about my traumatic experience. She asked to see the picture and laughed. "You must have asked her for a gua sha massage. It's nor-

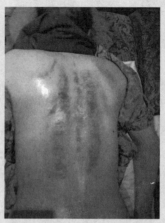

A cure for the common cold? The author's back after a gua sha *massage.*

mal in China. Look, I did it last weekend too." She showed me a picture of her back similarly violated. It turns out that since the masseuse noticed I had a cold, she offered me a gua sha massage as a treatment and I had inadvertently accepted.

That day I learned two valuable lessons: My strategy of smiling and nodding at anything I don't understand needed to be rethought, and TCM is not for me.

MYTHBUSTERS:
CHINA EDITION

Are Chinese bodies different?

This is a MYTH (according to the Western scientific community).

The idea that Chinese bodies are racially different from the rest of the world originates in a now-defunct multiregional theory of evolution.

In 1929, remains of a Homo erectus (an early form of Homo sapiens) were found in Zhoukoudian, China. The body was named "Peking Man," and he spawned theories that Chinese were evolved from a unique species of Homo sapiens.

This theory was made obsolete by the discovery of the remains of a 20,000-year-old woman in Africa. The consensus in the scientific community now is that all modern humans are direct descendants from African Homo sapiens.

Traditional Chinese Medicine

Scientists believe that some adventurous Homo sapiens left the African continent earlier than others. They traveled to Asia, interbred with primitive Homo sapiens breeds native to the continent, gave birth to Peking Man, and then they all went extinct. Chinese people today would still be directly descended from African Homo sapiens.

Yet there is still a community of Chinese scientists, notably Professor Wu Xinzhi of the Chinese Academy of Science, who argue for the multiregional theory of evolution. Indeed, Chinese students today are taught that they are descended from Peking Man, and most Chinese reject the idea they are descended from Africans. This is where the idea that "Chinese bodies are different" comes from.

CHAPTER SEVEN

Guide to Apartment Hunting in Beijing

※

Most companies who hire foreigners will either provide housing for you once you arrive in China, or pay for you to stay in a hotel until you find your own accommodation.

If you choose not to accept the housing, most schools are willing to negotiate giving you a salary increase in compensation. Then you will need to find your own place. The good news is that apartment hunting in Beijing is not much different from apartment hunting anywhere else in the world. You go on a website, look at the available apartments, see their price and location, take a tour and decide if you like it. The bad news is that you have to do all of this in Mandarin.

APARTMENT HUNTING ON THE BEIJINGER

There is one exception: A common way for expats to find housing in Beijing is through the classified section of our local expat magazine The Beijinger (www.thebeijinger.com/classifieds). The obvious benefit of doing this is that you can

A NOTE ON "HOUSING INCLUDED" JOB OFFERS

Before you accept, be aware that free housing can sometimes mean "cheapest apartment our company could find, never mind that it is overrun with cockroaches and also it is a three-hour train ride from our school." Don't accept any offers of housing until you have seen the apartment with your own eyes, and made sure that you can deal with the subway commute during peak rush hour every day for the next year without wanting to jump onto the tracks.

conduct your apartment-hunting in English, and you will most likely end up with other foreigners as roommates, who can help you adjust to life in China.

The negative is that since expat websites are targeted at expats, you will have to pay the foreigner tax—take what a Chinese person would pay and double the amount. It is common practice for unscrupulous vendors to overcharge expats based on the mistaken notion that all foreigners are rich (if only!). A room you could find for RMB 1000 a month on a Chinese website will now cost RMB 2000. The Beijinger is filled with agents who prey on foreigners who have no idea how much an apartment is supposed to cost and grossly overcharge for accommodations.

If you decide the convenience of apartment hunting in English and having foreign roommates is worth paying extra money, look for ads posted by expats themselves. Listings with "NO AGENT FEE" in the title that means you will be dealing with the other roommates directly instead of going through an agent. This will cut off the middleman and rent should be lower, though still more than a local would pay.

The other disadvantage of The Beijinger is that it considerably limits your housing options. Although there are hundreds of apartment listed at any time, most of them are listed by agents. After you filter out the agents and apartments too far for your commute, there will not be many rooms left.

HOW TO RENT AN APARTMENT THE CHINESE WAY

Fortunately, Chinese real estate websites are thriving and easy to navigate if you can read Mandarin. If you can't, find a Chinese friend or colleague and ask for their help. There are several major real estate websites in China and each has a different section for every major city. You just need to pick which neighborhood you want to live in (you can even pick which subway or bus stop you want to live close to), your budget, and you will find hundreds of listings. As always in China, watch out for scams. Many ads will put a beautiful picture of a completely different apartment in the listing. Be smart — if the listing shows a spacious, decorated apartment in the central business district of Beijing for only RMB 1000/month, it's probably fake.

Here are some of the most popular websites for house hunting:

- **Fang:** www.fang.com
- **Juwai:** www.juwai.com
- **Ganji:** www.ganji.com

These websites will put you in touch with real estate agents, who will show you around. These agents are less predatory than the ones on The Beijinger, because they are used to dealing with Chinese people who understand how the market works. Still, stick to your budget no matter what the agent says — he will push very hard to get you to stay in a more expensive apartment.

You can also go straight to an agent, though it's a good idea to check out the real estate websites first so you have a general idea of how much you should be paying for an apartment in any given neighborhood. There are two major real estate agencies in China and they have offices all over Beijing. Just walk into any of their offices (recognizable by their ubiquitous logos), state your budget and requirements, and let them show you around. You will need to be able to speak Mandarin, or bring along a Chinese friend.

Typical morning in a Chinese metro station.

- **我爱我家 (Wo Ai Wo Jia):** www.5i5j.com

- **链家 (Lianjia):** www.lianjia.com   LIONJIO.链家

PRICE

When people list Beijing as among the most expensive cities in the world, they are referring to housing prices. Renting an apartment will be your biggest expenditure in China. You can lower the price if you are willing to compromise on quality and location. Extending your commute and taking the subway can drastically cut costs — but keep in mind that commuters on the subway during rush hour somehow reach a liquefied state where they can squeeze their body to fit into every nook and cranny of the carriage until there is not a millimeter of space devoid of human flesh. If you like breathing you probably won't like Chinese subway commutes.

It's best to live close enough to your school that you can ride a motorbike or walk every day. Apartments in Chinese compounds are much cheaper than apartments in Western residential areas. Central neighborhoods are more expensive than the outskirts of the city.

WHICH NEIGHBORHOOD SHOULD I LIVE IN?

The most important consideration when picking your neighborhood should be your daily commute. Ideally you want to live somewhere close enough to your work that there is no need to take the subway — you can either walk, bike, or take a scooter. This can cover a relatively large area in central Beijing, however, so you will have some flexibility. Here is an introduction to the most popular expat neighborhoods in Beijing:

Dongzhimen

Possibly the most popular neighborhood for foreigners. Ideally located in the center of Beijing between the business district and the historic area.

Pros:

- Great location. Walkable both to Sanlitun and to Gulou
- Many Western-style shops, restaurants and shopping malls
- Many local Chinese shops and restaurants
- Close to Gui Jie (Ghost Street), one of the most famous streets in Beijing for authentic spicy Chinese food—hot pot, Peking Duck, noodles, etc.
- Apartment complexes feel very authentic. Expect to see old women dancing on the square while their husbands smoke and play card games nearby

Cons:

- The downside of authentic Chinese apartment complexes is that they are often old and run-down
- Rent is high relative to neighborhoods with few foreigners

Gulou

Gulou is both historic and hipster. Mostly made up of hutong houses and bell towers, it has a vibrant dining and nightlife scene.

THE ROSETTA STONE
CHINGLISH EDITION

Hutong (胡同, pinyin: hútòng)

Hutong can refer either to a traditional, gray-shingled house typical of northern China (especially Beijing) or neighborhoods and alleyways comprised of such houses.

Hutongs are fast disappearing, replaced by wide boulevards and modern buildings, but the government has designated certain neighborhoods in central Beijing as protected historic areas.

Hutongs are popular with poor Chinese who can't afford modern housing, and hipster expats who romanticize living in the past.

E.g., "Living in a hutong sounded like a great idea during the summer, but now it's December and I wish I had heating and an indoor bathroom."

Pros:

- You can live in the beautiful traditional hutong houses
- Gulou is fairly central. You can easily bike to Sanlitun, the CBD, and other popular neighborhoods

Hutong alley scene.

- Excellent drinking scene, with many bars that cater to expats (i.e., no fake alcohol)
- Good restaurants, of both the fine dining and hole-in-the-wall type
- People who go to Gulou tend to be in-the-know about Beijing, so it attracts long-term expats instead of tourists and exchange students

Cons:

- High rent for old, rundown apartment buildings
- Living in a hutong is nice in theory, but they can be cold, drafty, and dark in the winter months. Not to everyone's taste

- There is a downside to bars that don't serve fake alcohol — drinks are similarly priced as in the West

Sanlitun/CBD area

Most multinational companies and embassies have their offices in the Sanlitun/CBD (central business district) area. The slickest, most modern neighborhood in Beijing.

Pros:

- SLT/CBD is almost indistinguishable from a Western city in terms of apartments, facilities, gyms, food and bar options

Sanlitun on a remarkably quiet night — it is usually packed with pedestrians.

- Best place in Beijing to shop for Western brands
- Right in the center of Beijing, not far from the historic area and Tiananmen Square

Cons:

- The fact it is almost indistinguishable from a Western city could be seen as a con by some
- Very yuppie
- Most expensive area to live. Expect to pay at least 3,500 RMB/month. On the bright side, the apartment complexes are clean and modern
- Very expat-y. It's not uncommon to walk down the street and find that Chinese people are the minority

Shuangjing

Shuangjing is the neighborhood for people who want the Sanlitun experience without the Sanlitun prices.

Pros:

- Cheaper rent than in the CBD/Sanlitun area — expect to pay about 1000 RMB a month less for a similar apartment
- Not far from Sanlitun/CBD area. Four stops away on Line 10, easily bikeable
- Good dining and bar options

- Big shopping mall with Western brands
- Many gyms and fitness centers

Cons

- Far from Gulou/Dongzhimen area
- A bit soulless—no historic areas, no cultural sites, not much of a vibrant downtown area

Wudaokou

Wudaokou is Beijing's college town. There are seven major universities in the area, including China's two most famous: Tsinghua University and Peking University.

Pros:

- Very young, active neighborhood, with lots of bars and restaurants
- Very international—Chinese universities attract large numbers of African, Asian, and Western students
- The universities have gyms, parks, swimming pools, basketball courts, tennis courts, and other facilities that you can use at a fairly cheap price
- Because it's a student area, drink prices are low. Many of the nightclubs will let you in and give you six free drinks if you are a foreigner

Cons

- The alcohol in the various bars and clubs is usually fake — if you wake up the next day feeling like you consumed half a liter of antifreeze the night before, it's probably because you did (see chapter: "Pollution and other hazards")

- Can be very loud, rowdy, and crowded on popular going out nights

- Far from the rest of Beijing. If you want to visit the historic areas such as Tiananmen Square and Sanlitun,, you will have to take a subway for 40 minutes-1 hour

- Renting an apartment in this area is expensive. Expect to pay 3000 RMB+ a month

Others

These are only five of the neighborhoods in the sprawling megalopolis that is Beijing. They are the most popular with foreigners, which mean they are the most expensive. If you are under a strict budget, you should branch out of these areas and find a fully Chinese neighborhood. The lower rent will come at the price of longer commute and a less expat-friendly lifestyle (i.e., few cafes or Western restaurants, shopping not so accessible, more staring on the part of Chinese unused to seeing foreigners). But some expats like the more immersive experience and greater opportunities to mingle with Chinese people.

CONTRACT

Most likely you will be dealing with a Chinese landlord, and as such your contract will be entirely in Mandarin. Have a trusted friend or colleague translate for you if you can't understand. You should be looking for the following:

- Start date and end date. Is there possibility to extend the lease at the end?

- What happens in case the landlords decide to sell the apartment during your tenancy. It's not unheard of for a tenant to move into an apartment only to be told a month later it's been sold and they have four months to vacate.

- What furniture and appliances are listed as belonging to the apartment, and if they match what is really there

- How much notice should be given if either the landlord or tenant wishes to cancel the contract

- Rent payment: How much and what day of the month should it be paid? What are the penalties for late payment?

MAINTENANCE

It is the duty of your landlord to provide maintenance for the apartment, but it is not guaranteed that he will do so. Make sure you have the contact details of your landlord (not an agent) and call him to alert if anything needs to be fixed.

Expect that he will tell you he will send someone to fix the problem "soon," which could mean in an hour or never. If it's a minor problem you can fix yourself or pay someone cheaply to fix for you, it is probably worth taking that route instead.

DEPOSITS

You will generally have to pay between one and six months' deposit when you move into an apartment (the norm is you put down one month's rent as deposit, and pay the first three months' rent). At the end of your stay, landlords will try to keep as much of your deposit as possible, blaming you for any imperfection in the apartment, no matter how unlikely it is that you are the one who caused it. When you move into a new apartment make sure to document everything and have pictures ready to show your landlord at the end of your stay to prove you are not responsible for the problems. He might keep your deposit anyway, and there won't be much you can do about it. Foreigners don't really have access to legal aid in China. Try to build a good relationship with your landlord throughout your stay—pay your rent on time, don't bother him with minor problems you can sort out yourself, follow the rules, and hope he will treat you right in the end.

REGISTRATION

It is the duty of landlords to register with the local police station foreigners living in their apartments, but they will often neglect to do so (and then lie about it). To be safe, you should ask your landlord for the address of the local police station and go register yourself.

MAID SERVICE

China's massive population might make your daily commute unpleasant, but it does have one benefit: cheap cost of labor. This means the majority of middleclass people can afford maid service, and most foreigners employ an ayi to come wash their house once a week at the price of RMB 50 per hour (equivalent $8 per hour). Ayis will sweep, mop, wash and iron clothes, wash dishes, and can even cook dinner. Having a maid is a privilege few millennials in the West can afford so take advantage of it.

THE ROSETTA STONE
CHINGLISH EDITION

Ayi (阿姨, pinyin: āyí, lit: aunt)

Cleaner employed in private homes.

E.g. "Who knew there were so many cockroaches in this apartment? I wonder if it's because I haven't done the dishes in a month. Thank God the ayi is coming tomorrow!"

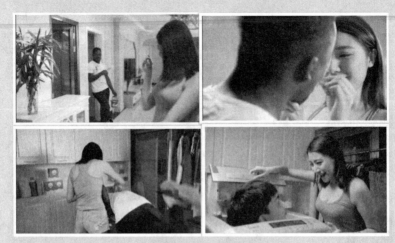

Hmm, could this possibly be racist?

RACISM

A Chinese TV advertisement made headlines around the world in 2016 for its remarkably unsubtle racism. In the ad for Qiaobi laundry detergent, a black man approaches a Chinese woman in a laundromat and wolf-whistles. She responds by doing what anyone would do in this scenario, and shoves him in the washing machine after stuffing his mouth with laundry detergent. He comes out Chinese, and the two lovebirds smile, presumably ready to live happily ever after.

The video's blatant symbolism astonished Westerners, who reposted it on Reddit and YouTube, where it quickly went viral. It drew the attention of CNN, BBC, The New York Times, Buzzfeed, and basically every prominent Western media organization, who all headlined their articles with some different variation of "Wow, this is the most racist thing ever!"

When Qiaobi realized how much international outrage the advertisement sparked, it released a statement saying that, "We meant nothing but to promote the product, and we had never thought about the issue of racism. The foreign media might be too sensitive about the ad."

This was not the most heartfelt of apologies, and did little to placate critics (Qiaobi eventually released another, more sensitive one). Yet, "We had never thought about the issue of racism" offers a concise summary of Chinese attitudes toward racial relations. Most Chinese people are simply not aware of the concept of racism. There is no culture of racial awareness or political correctness in China, in part because the country has not had to deal with the same history of violent racism that Western countries are trying to atone for.

China has its own minority races. The government officially recognizes 55 minorities, which altogether make up close to nine percent of the total population. These minorities are officially protected by the government, and discrimination is illegal. Yet Chinese minorities do not look significantly different from the majority Han. For the most part they cannot be distinguished by appearance alone, unlike in the United States or England where it is often easy to tell the difference between whites and non-whites. China looks largely homogeneous, except for foreigners.

I am not qualified to discuss how much racism and discrimination minorities face within China. Evidence suggests there is some.

However, there is a clear racism issue with regards to non-Chinese people, especially non-white ones.

When it comes to white people, China suffers from both arrogance and an inferiority complex. While most Chinese would agree that China is unquestionably the most superior country in the world, they regard Western countries' economic, technological, and cultural achievements with a mixture of admiration and jealousy. In the eyes of most Chinese, Western = white, and white people are extended respect by virtue of being associated with the West, no matter if they are American or Russian or South African.

By contrast, there is a great deal of ignorance surrounding non-whites. For many Chinese, the recent influx of Africans to China is the first time they have ever encountered a dark-skinned person. Unfortunately, their first reaction is often fear.

The media plays a role in perpetuating these views. My students would often say things like, "I am scared of black people. They are very violence." When asked to elaborate, they would respond by saying black actors in foreign movies were usually gangsters, they had watched news reports about shootings and gang violence in the U.S., and learned about war and poverty in African nations. If they have never had contact with a black person in their life, and all they see in fiction and media is about black violence and poverty, can they be blamed for forming a negative impression of black people? With regard to other races, in general the standard is that if they are not white or East Asian, they are looked down upon, for similar reasons of stereotyping and ignorance.

It does not help that Chinese beauty standards emphasize whiteness of skin, with darkness being associated with poverty. All these factors conflate to a premium placed on whiteness when it comes to hiring foreigners for any position, particularly teaching. It is difficult to find exact statistics on this issue, but anecdotal evidence strongly suggests that parents prefer having white teachers for their children. Even if the white foreigner is Russian and speaks English as a second language, he will be favored over an African-American, Asian-American, or Indian-American most of the time.

This is not a universal rule. More serious English language schools (think the big companies like English First, New Oriental, Wall Street English, etc.) require a US, UK, Canadian, or Australian passport to be hired, and will usually not discriminate on race as long as you meet this qualification. In Tier 1 cities where Chinese people are getting used to foreigners, people are starting to understand that Western does not mean white, which makes them more open to hiring non-whites as teachers.

And Chinese people do seem open to changing their views regarding black people when presented with an opportunity. The NBA is hugely popular among young Chinese men, most of whom have a favorite player (usually black) whose praises they sing when writing essays and posting on social media. Once black teachers are hired, their students tend to be pleased at the novelty and curious to get to know more about them. I have had two black friends—one British and one American—work as English teachers, and both were hugely popular with their students and regarded as an asset by their company. In day-to-day life they were mostly treated the same as whites, other than some extra staring on the subway and questions regarding their hair. The situation is improving.

Yet unfortunately it is a fact that most Chinese parents do prefer white teachers, particularly in Tier 2 cities and below where ignorance regarding foreign cultures is deeply entrenched. If you are non-white and considering teaching English in China, understand that you will face extra obstacles and challenges compared to a white person. But it is far from impossible to succeed as a black person in China, and you might find it rewarding to help Chinese people rethink their stereotypes.

CHAPTER EIGHT

Job Hunting in Beijing

TEACHING JOBS

By far the easiest and most lucrative jobs for foreigners in Beijing are English teaching jobs. A typical ad might say:

"Looking for Kindergarden teacher!! Must be a good storyteller and fun-loving! Attractive salary! Native speakers only! Work visa provided!"

It is common practice for Chinese people to include a photo of themselves in their resume. If you are white, it would be particularly to your advantage to do so. Chinese companies favor white teachers. If you possess a passport from the US, UK, Australia, New Zealand, or Canada, also make that very clear in your resume. The highest salaries go to native English speakers.

Some employers will sponsor your work visa, others will not. Usually if the company offers a work visa they will clearly state so in the job advertisement.

For a teaching job, you should be looking for a salary in the 13k-20k RMB a month range. The highest salaries will go to native English speakers who are graduates of top universities, majored in the field of education, or who already have several years teaching experience. If you tick all these boxes you might even be able to make up to 30k a month, which is a salary most Chinese can only dream of.

NON-TEACHING JOBS

It is possible to find jobs outside of education in China, but they are considerably fewer and generally they do not pay as well. For a non-teaching job, expect to make 8k to 12k at the very most. Chinese companies have little incentive to hire a foreigner who speaks poor Mandarin when a Chinese employee could do a better job at a lower salary. It is also much harder to get a work visa for a non-teaching jobs — because of Chinese protectionist laws, the company must prove that it is necessary to hire a foreigner for this position instead of a native.

If you speak upper intermediate to advanced Mandarin (HSK 5), you might be able to find work. Rightly or wrongly, there is a stereotype in China that foreigners are more creative and innovative than locals, and companies like to hire foreigners to offer "a Western perspective," whatever that means. Typical non-teaching jobs for expats in China include translators, editors, and foreign recruiters.

(To be clear, this section does not apply to high-skilled employees — lawyers, engineers, managers, etc. These are usually hired from outside China by a recruiter, or transferred here within their company. I am talking about young university graduates with little work experience who came to China to teach English.)

Visa

To get a work permit for a non-teaching job, you need to have either two years work experience relevant to the position or a master's degree. This is stricter than getting a work permit for a teaching job, for which two years post-graduate work experience in any field is acceptable.

Before accepting a non-teaching job offer, be aware that although Chinese companies will assure you that they can provide a work visa, often the HR employee making the promise has no idea what obtaining a work permit entails and might not be able to follow through. A smaller company might be willing to let you work illegally on a tourist or business visa, but large multinational companies will usually not take that risk.

A note on face jobs

Chinese companies used to be willing to shell out a lot of money for the prestige of having a foreign employee to give them worldly credibility. As the number of foreigners in China rises, it is becoming increasingly difficult to impress Chinese people with your foreign face and foreign passport, and this phenomenon is disappearing. Particularly in

I was offered a job at a large multinational firm, but ultimately couldn't get a visa due to a lack of relevant work experience. The HR manager said they used to allow expats to work on the wrong visa, but this was becoming impossible and they were no longer willing to take this risk (and if it weren't for that bureaucratic snafu, this book would never have been written).

The centerpiece of President Xi Jinping's administration has been a severe crackdown on corruption. The police once made money off taking bribes from corporations to turn a blind eye to illegally employed foreigners. Now they make money off stiff penalties on corporations who are not following the law to the letter.

international cities like Beijing and Shanghai, being foreign is no longer enough to guarantee you a high salary.

Yet there is still a market for "face jobs." A face job is when a company hires you only because you are foreign. They do not have any work for you to do, and most likely you will just be trotted out for company events or made to sit in on business meetings. Outside of that you will be sitting around twiddling your thumbs.

A face job might sound good on the surface — get paid to browse the internet all day is many young adult's dream come true. But I've met several face job employees, and they complain how mind-numbingly boring it is to have nothing to do for 9 hours a day, and regret that they do not have the opportunity to build up their skills. Career-wise, face jobs are a waste of time, though they will allow you to save up a decent nest egg.

How to spot a face job

- The job title is vague and grandiose; i.e. "Assistant to the President" or "Vice Chairman of the Company"
- The job posting specifies ethnicity or gender preferred
- The salary is high — something like 18k a month
- The job duties are vague: "Looking for creative, enthusiastic assistant to the chairman! Help manage day-to-day operations! Help with public relations of company!"

If a job seems too good to be true, it probably is. Why would a Chinese company hire a young graduate with no skills, who can't speak Mandarin, to become vice chairman of their company? As the Chinese proverb goes, "Pancakes don't fall from the sky."

CAUTIONARY TALE

A friend accepted a job in a martial arts company that offered her 18k a month to be "Assistant to the President." She was promised business trips all over China and opportunities to work with the media promoting the company.

When she was hired her (married) boss took her with him to all his business meetings and dinners, often staying with her until 10 or 11 P.M. He offered her Hermes perfumes and other luxury gifts. He found excuses to touch her and made comments about how attractive he found foreign girls. Her colleagues began joking that she was the new girlfriend—apparently this was a common pattern of behavior with him.

Finally he invited himself into her hotel room during a business trip and forced himself on her. After this he lost interest, and her working hours and responsibilities were drastically cut. She was eventually turned into an English teacher for his primary school son.

This story is not particularly unusual in China, which has lax sexual harassment laws and few recourses for women dealing with overly friendly bosses. Western women, with our reputation for "openness," are particularly vulnerable.

NO, I DON'T WANT
TO BUILD A SNOWMAN

I was once selected to judge a talent show produced by CCTV, China's national broadcast company. The show is the largest English-language talent show in the world, and goes by the name of "Star of Outlook" (is it ironic that an English talent show has a badly-translated Chinglish name? Yes.).

Any illusion I had that working for a TV show would be glamorous was quickly dispelled. Every weekend the judges and contestants were summoned to a large resort hotel in the suburbs of Beijing. Our job was to select the applicants who got onto the TV show, sort of like Simon Cowell, if Simon Cowell didn't get to speak and didn't go on TV. So, it was Simon Cowell's job with all the fun bits taken out and only the part where you have to listen to awful singing for hours left in.

Twelve hours a day we sat in a sweltering theater room under powerful floodlights serenaded, one-by-one, by an endless sea of little girls dressed like Elsa who showed us a thousand and one artistic interpretations of a single song: "Let It Go." The Elsas, in turn, were alternated by hundreds of little boys dressed like snowmen singing "Do you

(continued)

Want to Build a Snowman?" (this was the year after Frozen came out). A few bold nonconformists sang "Twinkle Twinkle Little Star," though I suspect that was because their English level was too low to sing anything more complex. This went on until we all wanted to do like van Gogh and cut off our ears. It was like hell had Frozen over.

That was the singing component of the show. There was also a speech component, with the prompt: "Tell us something about Chinese culture."

The prompt was unimaginative; the speeches were tedious. Every single one began with the stock phrase: "China has 5,000 years of history." It was so ridiculous that by the end the contestants would feel compelled to add, "As we all know" at the start. "As we all know... China has 5,000 years of history."

"YES," the judges wanted to scream, "WE ALL KNOW THAT CHINA HAS 5000 YEARS OF HISTORY. WE GET IT. 5000 YEARS. VERY IMPRESSIVE. NOW CAN YOU PLEASE LOOK INTO THOSE 5,000 YEARS AND FIND SOMETHING ELSE TO TALK ABOUT?"

From "China has 5,000 years of history" the speeches would veer into one of three directions: tea, calligraphy, or Kung Fu. Little girls daintily showed us how a tea ceremony is conducted (the wily ones would try to score extra points by offering us samples) and little boys showed us their best Jackie Chan impression. Many of the speeches were clearly plagiarized off the internet, since different contestants repeated each other word for word.

We were supposed to work for eight hours a day but there were so many contestants we ran over by hours each time. Occasionally we could convince the producers to give us a short bathroom break, though they agreed with eye rolls and sighs, as if we were demanding foot massages. I did this for several months until I couldn't take it anymore and used my hard-earned money to book a flight to Vietnam. Since then merely hearing the words "Let It Go" gives me a migraine, and whenever anyone tries to tell me that China has 5,000 years of history it takes all my willpower not to tell them that China can take its ancient heritage and shove it up its you-know-what.

HOW TO FIND JOBS ONLINE

If you enter Beijing as a rogue agent (i.e. not affiliated to an agency), or if you want to find another job once your first contract has ended, you can easily find work online. Here are some websites to help you with your job search:

Echinacities (jobs.echinacities.com)

Echinacities has possibly the highest number of listings for jobs for foreigners. The website is entirely in English, and recruiters from all over the country post open positions there.

How to use the website

The numbers of jobs listed on Echinacities is slightly over-whelming. You can filter based on city, part-time or full-time, salary range, internship or freelance, and job category (HR, engineering, education, hospitality, finance, etc.)

To respond to an ad, you have to sign up on the website and submit your resume. Unfortunately, you cannot upload your own, so you have to fill out the online questionnaire and the website will create one for you. Use of Echinacities to search for jobs is free.

Points

Echinacities offers some extra features that can be exchanged for 20 or 30 points. Those features include promoting your resume on the website so recruiters can easily find you, instead of you having to apply for jobs individually. You can also see which companies have checked out your resume, and how many applicants there are for any given position.

To earn points, you need to engage with the website outside of the job section. If you write a blog post, you earn 15 points. If you comment on a blog post, you earn 2 points. If you upload a picture of yourself, you earn 5 points.

There is a maximum number of points you can earn each day through comments, presumably to avoid people flooding comment sections to increase points. The comment section of Echinacities is weird — a mix of people who clearly haven't read the post and just comment, "Great read thanks!" to earn points, and embittered expats who take any opportunity to go on a racist tangent.

The Beijinger (www.thebeijinger.com/classifieds/employment)

The classified section of our favorite local English-language magazine also offers a respectable selection of jobs for foreigners for both teaching and non-teaching positions. Similarly to Echinacities, on the Beijinger you can sort jobs by contract status (full-time, part-time, freelance) and employment area (teaching, IT, creative, secretarial). Additionally you can sort jobs by neighborhoods, so you can find a position with a short commute.

To apply for positions on The Beijinger you do not need to sign up to the website. The job posting will include an email address where you can send your resume and cover letter.

Chamber of Commerce

You might also have some luck looking at the American, British, or Australian Chamber of Commerce websites. If you are fluent in another language (German, Spanish, French, for example) you can also look at those countries' Chamber of Commerce websites.

Chamber of Commerce websites offer a limited selection of jobs, and often have higher requirements for qualifications. There are also many internships advertised, and few if any teaching positions. A typical Chamber of Commerce job posting is similar to something you would find on LinkedIn:

> *The Director, Security Risk Management-China will have overall responsibility for the SRM service line in China. The role includes origination, client relationships management, project management, developing proposal and case strategies, managing case budgets, and quality control of deliverables and leading the service line team. The scope for the Security Risk Management services includes delivery of consulting services with respect to Security Management, Crisis Response and Incident Management, Physical Security, Security Systems, Planning & Design, Threat & Vulnerability Risk Assessments, Gap Analysis, Emergency & Contingency Planning, Technical Surveillance Countermeasures and Crime Prevention Through Environmental Design (CPTED) principles and others.*

Basically, Chamber of Commerce websites are international companies looking for fluent speakers of their language to join their team. These jobs are generally more reputable and therefore the competition is fierce. Most postings will require applicants to be fluent in Mandarin.

Chamber of Commerce in China websites:

- American Chamber of Commerce: www.amchamchina.org
- British Chamber of Commerce: www.britishchamber.cn
- Australian Chamber of Commerce: austcham.org
- French Chamber of Commerce: www.ccifc.org
- German Chamber of Commerce: china.ahk.de

CHINESE RECRUITMENT WEBSITES

If you speak Mandarin, you might have some luck looking at Chinese job recruiting websites. These are the websites that Chinese people themselves use, and consequently the job postings are targeted at natives: You must be able to speak fluent Mandarin, and expect to receive a salary typical for a Chinese person in Beijing (around 6000RMB/month). If you want to perfect your Mandarin or acquire experience in a Chinese business environment, this is the way to go.

The following are the largest recruitment websites in China:

1. Zhaopin: www.zhaopin.com

2. 1job: www.51job.com

3. ChinaHR: www.chinahr.com/beijing

All of these websites are very active, and allow you to fil-ter the job similarly to Echinacities: contract type, employ-ment area, expected salary, etc.

CONCLUSION

It is very easy for a foreigner to be hired in China...as an English teacher. Other jobs are much more competitive. But if you are happy teaching English, you will never be unem-ployed for long in Beijing.

SQUARE DANCING

One of the most charming sights in China is a public square filled with dozens of old women bopping together to a beat from a nearby speaker. "Square dancing" is China's answer to water aerobics: a low-impact exercise method and a social outlet for the elderly community.

The music is forgettable—bland synthetic beats without any singing. The movements are simple and repetitive—no twerking. And yet there is something endearing about seeing these elderly women dancing together unself-consciously on a sunny day. Occasionally men will join the fun, and old couples will spin and twirl together, faces flushed and eyes twinkling.

The party sometimes gets out of control—these square dancers may not be young but they are wild and free. Working-age Chinese demanded square dancers be banned outdoors, complaining that they were being wakened at five in the morning by the sound of their revelry. For several months the country was gripped with tension as the elderly fought for their right to dance. A ceasefire was finally reached when the government restricted the volume at which music could be played and the hours when square dancers could meet.

For now, China's elderly continue to spin around gaily at dusk on a summer day, the last rays of the sun illuminating this charming tradition.

我 我 我 我 我 我
我 我

CHAPTER NINE

Learning Mandarin

※

O ne of the great things about moving to China is that you get to experience what it would be like to be an illiterate peasant in the sixteenth century. It is a disconcerting experience even if you're already a worldly and well-traveled person. Most countries use an alphabet, and even if you don't speak the local language, as you travel through Argentina you can guess that the building with the word "Restaurante" written on it is a restaurant, and the "Toilette" sign in a Parisian cafe means bathroom.

Not so in China. Once you get off the plane you will revert to an infantile state of total illiteracy. In some ways this can be good — you will be blind to the aggressively patriotic propaganda banners around the city exhorting citizens to "Love your country! Promote Chinese civilization! Unity is strength!" Yet being totally cut off from communication with the world around you can be alienating.

For this reason, even if you have no intention of spending more than a year in China and therefore see no point in pursuing the Herculean task of learning Mandarin, it's a good idea to take some basic language courses when you

A bit more complex than Spanish 101

arrive. The great thing about learning Mandarin is that Chinese people have very low expectations of foreigners' ability to speak their language — learn how to say, "Hello, I am American," and you can enjoy the enthusiastic praise of locals for the rest of your stay.

You might be content to stop once you've learned how to order beer and tell the taxi driver how to bring you home. Alternatively, you might find yourself drawn to this complex and poetic language and decide to pursue it further. You'll never know until you try. Just don't become one of those expats who come to China for a year and at the end of your contract decide to stay for "one more year!" and before you know it you've spent five years in China and still can't order spicy fish tofu. There's no excuse not to learn Mandarin as language teachers abound in the cities. Most expats choose either private tutors or attend language schools.

For private tutoring, prices range from RMB 50-150 per hour ($7-23) depending on qualifications and experience. This is more expensive than a class in a school, but it has the convenience that they will meet you at the time and location of your choice. You can also decide what material you want to study, whether you want to focus on speaking or writing, conversation or HSK.

Private tutors often advertise on notice boards in cafes frequented by Westerners, or expat websites. Look for someone who has majored in Teaching Chinese as a Foreign Language, but be aware it is common practice to exaggerate or outright lie about qualifications. Just because someone writes an advertisement stating they have years of experience teaching Mandarin at the best university in China doesn't mean it's true.

For that reason **schools can be a safer bet, as teachers in a Chinese language school will have gone through a vetting process before being hired.** Schools typically offer either private lessons or group classes. Prices can go as low as RMB 30 ($4.50) for an hour of group classes. Language schools also often offer cultural activities like excursions to

HANG LOOSE, DUMPLING DUDE

Chinese people have hand signs to communicate numbers less than ten. Making a fist means ten. Sticking out your thumb and curling your index fingers means seven. And the sign for six looks like this:

 It also happened that the dumplings I bought on my way to work every morning were six RMB. The vendor would make the sign for six at me, trying to tell me to pay six kuai. Being a stupid laowai I would smile and make the sign back. We waved our hands at each other until he got impatient and grabbed the money from me.

This went on for several weeks — him asking me to pay six kuais, me smiling cluelessly and flashing him the hang loose sign. I thought I had stumbled upon a very chill dumpling dude who wanted to send me good vibes.

Eventually my Chinese teacher went over the different signs for numbers, and I realized why dumpling dude and all his friends looked at me like I had brain damage when I walked by his little shop and flashed him the "hang loose" sign.

the Great Wall or hot pot dinners. This can be a good way to learn more about Chinese culture and make friends.

When picking a school, look for small class sizes (four to five people) as this will give you more opportunities to practice your speaking and communicate with the others. Make sure there are different levels available so you are grouped with people of approximately your ability. It's a waste of time to sit in a class with students who are still learning how to say "The scenery in Beijing is very beautiful" when you want to discuss the latest Chow Yun-Fat movie; alternatively, taking part in a class where you need to stop your classmates and teacher after every sentence to ask them to explain their meaning is very damaging to your ego.

Mandarin is a famously difficult language to learn—nonnative speakers agonize over memorizing characters and learning to speak with tones. If your goal is mastery of a foreign language in a short time, move to Spain. However, getting to the stage where you can have basic conversation with taxi drivers, waiters, and shopkeepers is achievable within a few months. The ability to communicate with people around you is a blessing you do not appreciate until you lose it. Invest the time to learn basic conversational Mandarin and watch China become one hundred percent more livable.

SELECTION OF MANDARIN SCHOOLS IN BEIJING

Hutong School
Address: Zhongyu Plaza, room 1501, 15th floor A6 Gongti Beilu, 100027 Chaoyang District Beijing 北京市朝阳区工体北路甲6号中宇大厦1501室100027
Email: www.hutong-school.com

The Culture Yard
Address: 10 Shique Hutong, Dongcheng, Beijing
Website: www.cultureyard.net

That's Mandarin
Address: 新中街乙12号4号楼一层, Dongcheng, Beijing, China
Website: www.thatsmandarin.com

Capital Mandarin School
Address: China, Beijing Shi, Chaoyang Qu, 高碑店西店村26号楼号8门
Website: www.capitalmandarin.com

Global Village School
Address: China, Beijing, Haidian, Zhongguancun E Rd, 华清嘉园7-6号华清商务会馆501 邮政编码: 100083

Website: this school does not have a website. It is worth checking out as one of the cheapest options for learning Mandarin in Beijing—only 36 RMB for an hour of class! Located in the center of Wudakou close to the McDonald's.

Purple Bamboo School

Wudaokou address: Room 327—328, Longhu Tangning One Building 2-2B, Zhongguancun East Road, Haidian District 海淀区中关村东路16号院（龙湖唐宁One小区）2-2B，327,328室

Gulou address: Gulou West Street, No.3 Ganlu Huong, Xicheng District 西城区鼓楼西大街甘露胡同3号

Guomao address: NEST CAFE, No.29 Baiziwan Road, Chaoyang District 朝阳区百子湾路29号，巢咖啡

Website: None

THE HSK TEST

Many expats come to China with the express purpose of learning Mandarin. In that case, you will probably need to take the HSK (汉语水平考试 Hànyǔ Shuǐpíng Kǎoshì). This is the only standardized test of Mandarin proficiency, and it is common for employment or university applications to require candidates to have a level of HSK5 or above.

HSK tests reading, writing, and listening but not speaking. Each level is twice as difficult as the last, meaning you are expected to know twice as many words as the level below. HSK1 and HSK2 are for beginners. HSK3 and HSK4 are for intermediate. HSK5 and HSK6 are advanced.

Each section has a maximum score of 100. Tests are held in China and abroad, usually once a month. Studying for the HSK is a good investment of time if you intend to apply for universities or jobs that require Mandarin. It's an objective way to demonstrate a certain level of proficiency.

Keep in mind, however, that spoken and written Mandarin differ widely. This isn't an issue at the beginner or intermediate level, where you are learning such basic words that the divergence is not great. Once you get to intermediate-advanced or advanced, however, the vocabulary and grammar becomes entirely different. If you focus exclusively on the HSK your speaking will suffer—imagine a Chinese person coming up to you and addressing you in Shakespearean English. While you would understand their meaning you would wonder why they didn't learn to talk like a normal person. Speaking with your HSK vocabulary will make you sound similarly strange to a Chinese person. The average Chinese doesn't know what the HSK is and will assess your Mandarin ability by how well you speak, so it's important to pursue both conversational and HSK classes.

学書者而入二王人物

斷其秦之以必點佳

子實二氣古法多法

凡夫自多淺者惟

求少加乎法猶而

夫筆而時代歷之

不称之古之至而但

可知于江維當尤大為

楊為也

CHAPTER TEN

Mastering Mandarin

⁂

Mandarin is a poetic, ambiguous, and opaque language. Understanding a Chinese novel requires extensive knowledge of Chinese history, philosophy, and literature, as Chinese literature is deeply incestuous and authors quote and reference each other constantly. Chinese literary style is totally alien from a Western perspective. Ideas are not expressed directly, and writers rely on metaphors and similes to convey their meaning.

Part of the charm of learning Mandarin rests on its profound foreignness. Once you get to the stage where you begin to decipher novels and newspapers you feel like you are on the verge of discovering a whole new way of thinking and processing the world, and to turn back now would mean wasting the monumental effort it took to get there. At that stage learning Mandarin becomes addictive—you just want to take one more hit, memorize one more character, learn one more proverb. You might begin to feel like your weekly two hours of Chinese classes is limiting your ability to reach your full potential, and it's time to totally dedicate yourself to language learning.

CHINESE VS. ENGLISH METHODS OF EXPRESSION

Look at Xi Jinping's grand announcement in 2014 of an anti-corruption campaign that would target "the tigers and the flies." Does China suffer from an epidemic of unscrupulous wildlife? No, the name is a reference to the ambition to squash corruption all the way from the powerful officials in the Politburo (the tigers) to the insignificant party members at the provincial level (the flies). It's hard to imagine a US president announcing his objectives in such an indirect way, but this is a common method of expression in China.

If that's the case, consider enrolling in a Mandarin program at an accredited university in China. Most of them are reasonably priced and will do much more to improve your language skills than memorizing a few flashcards in between teaching kindergarten and hitting the bar. The following is a list of some of the most famous programs.

FOR MANDARIN BEGINNERS

China's two most famous universities are Peking University and Tsinghua University. Both have beautiful historic campuses in the Beijing neighborhood of Wudakou and attract the nation's most promising students. Admissions into either Tsinghua or Peking U is a high honor that most Chinese students can only dream of, but it is easily accessible for foreign students who wish to take part in the universities' Chinese language programs.

Requirements

- Must possess a non-Chinese passport (or be a resident of Hong Kong, Taiwan, or Macao)
- Between 18 and 45 years of age
- High school graduate
- In good health (with a medical certificate to prove it)

Tsinghua University Chinese Language Course

Tsinghua University's Chinese Language Course offers classes for eight levels ranging from beginner to advanced. The course runs on a semester basis, each 18 weeks long: Spring semester runs from mid-February to the end of June, and autumn semester runs from early September to mid-January. The program admits around 200 students each semester, and most stay only one semester though there is

DO YOU LIKE TO 打飞机?

One of the most embarrassing stories from my time as a teacher happened very early in my career. At the time my students were still too shy around me to do more than stare at me with wide eyes and occasionally giggle nervously.

As a way to get the students talking, I asked them to tell me about the most popular video games in China. They listed the universal favorites: League of Legends, Minecraft, World of Warcraft. One boy said he really enjoyed "dafeiji." The whole class burst into laughter.

"What is dafeiji?" I asked.

"It is popular China video game. All the boys play," he answered. There was more laughter.

I figured it must be a popular Chinese game that hadn't made it internationally yet. So for the next few months, whenever the topic of video games came up I would say something like, "Have you played dafeiji recently? I know you guys really like dafeiji." Each time they had a fit of laughter. My students were delighted whenever I displayed any insider knowledge of China, so this did not strike me as suspect; I thought I had impressed them with my familiarity with Chinese popular culture, and mentioned "dafeiji" in several of my classes.

One day, after I had again mentioned "the popular Chinese video game dafeiji," a student asked me:

"Teacher, do you know what dafeiji means?"

"No, but I know it's a Chinese video game."

"Teacher, dafeiji means..." he was too embarrassed to say it out loud and pointed to the dictionary on his phone. "Dafeiji" translated to "hit the plane; slang term for masturbation."

"So when you've been asking us if we like to dafeiji, you've been asking... you know." He blushed and the whole class giggled.

"What?! Of course I had no idea that that's what it meant! Why didn't any of you tell me this before? You must have realized I was making a mistake."

"Well, you know, Americans are very open. We thought it was very strange in the beginning, but then we thought maybe this is a normal question for a teacher to ask in America. But I wanted to ask you if you know the meaning, just to be sure."

I was too embarrassed to approach the topic with my other classes, so I never mentioned the subject of dafeiji again, not even to explain my mistake. I may have inadvertently created a generation of young Chinese who believe American teachers like to ask their students if they've masturbated recently.

the option to extend. There are twenty hours of classes a week: four hours each morning from Monday to Friday.

Classes offered:

Mandatory: Speaking, Listening Comprehension, Comprehensive Chinese, Extensive Reading, Newspaper Reading, Classical Chinese, Hot Topics, Writing, Pronunciation, Reading Aloud, and Discussion

Electives: Students have the option to add elective courses on top of the regular twenty hours for a fee. These are the electives offered:

Chinese Character (elementary), Chinese Character (intermediate-advanced), Pronunciation (elementary), Pronunciation (intermediate-advanced), Chinese Calligraphy, Chinese Painting, Chinese Songs, HSK Lessons, Taiji, Chinese Martial Arts, Chinese Er-hu, etc.

Advanced speakers can also take: Chinese Culture, Business Chinese, Audio-Visual lessons, Classical Chinese, Grammar and Advanced Listening Comprehension.

Cost:

Tuition: 12,600 RMB per semester

Living: accommodation available on campus for RMB 80/day/person for single bed rooms and RMB 40/day/person for double bed rooms.

Contact

For more information, send an email to chinese@tsinghua. edu.cn or look at the program's website: is.tsinghua.edu.cn

Peking University Chinese Language Studies Program

Peking University offers a similar Chinese language program. The schedule is identical: twenty hours of class a week, four hours a day Monday-Friday. Students are divided into elementary, intermediate, or advanced levels at the beginning of the program. After successfully finishing the program, students receive an official transcript and a certificate of completion. Classes run on a semester basis, from September to January and February to June. Students cannot stay more than four semesters consecutively.

West Gate of Peking University

Classes offered:

Mandatory courses: Intensive Reading, Spoken Chinese, Pronunciation, Listening Comprehension and Video Course.

Elective courses: Chinese Folklore, Translation, Rhetoric, Writing, Newspaper Reading, Classical Chinese, and Selected Readings from Contemporary Chinese Literature, etc. All courses aim to improve the student's the ability to use Mandarin in real-life circumstances.

Tuition is higher than at Tsinghua's program because Peking offers additional extracurricular Chinese cultural and immersive activities. For example: visits to Mutianyu Great Wall, visit to Mountain Tai and Confucius's hometown, as well as trips to other provinces and cities of China.

Cost

Tuition: 18,000 RMB per semester

Accommodations: Students are not guaranteed on-campus accommodations, which means many students live in the nearby neighborhood of Wudaokou. An apartment in Wudaokou costs around 3000 RMB per month for a room in a shared flat.

Contact: For more information, refer to the program's website: english.pku.edu.cn/Admission/InternationalStudents/GeneralInformation

FOR INTERMEDIATE MANDARIN SPEAKERS

Inter-University Program for Chinese Language Studies, UC Berkeley

IUP is the most intensive Chinese-language program in Beijing, and one of the best Mandarin programs in the world. At the cost of $17,100 per academic year, it is also one of the most expensive. The program is run by UC Berkeley but takes place on the campus of Tsinghua University.

IUP prides itself on its small class sizes and immersive experience. The student to teacher ratio is guaranteed not to exceed 3:1 and every student has one hour of individual lessons a day. Students are not allowed to speak any language other than Mandarin while on IUP campus, and violation of this rule will result in a grade penalty. The organization has a wide network of contacts in Beijing, and regularly holds networking events for current students and alumni. Everyone I have met who took part in IUP agrees it was worth the cost since it improved their Mandarin dramatically and put them in contact with prominent members in the world of China business and research.

Admissions are more selective than for the Tsinghua and Peking language courses. Applicants must have two years of Mandarin college-level study or equivalent (basically, lower intermediate level), a good academic record, and must be currently enrolled in university or already graduated.

Courses offered: Colloquial Dialogues, Radio News, Radio Discussion, TV Reportage, Colloquial Language, Reading, Classical Chinese.

Cost

Tuition: Full year is $17,000, semester is $9,000, summer program is $5,000

Housing: Students can apply for the student dormitory at Tsinghua but are not guaranteed a spot. Tsinghua dorms cost RMB 80/day/person for single bed rooms and RMB 40/day/person for double bed rooms. Otherwise, a room in a shared flat in Wudaokou costs about 3000 RMB/month.

Scholarships: If you are interested in the program but the cost is too steep, here is a list of organizations that offer language-study scholarships at IUP: Freeman-Asia Program, The Blakemore Foundation Fellowship, National Security Education Program, Social Science Research Council.

Contact: For more information, see IUP's website at ieas.berkeley.edu/iup

Council on International Educational Exchange at Peking University

Peking and Tsinghua have a long-standing rivalry, and Peking's answer to IUP is the Council on International Educational Exchange (CIEE) Mandarin program. CIEE is more expensive and lacks IUP's prestige, but it is also a reputable program for intermediate level students who wish to quickly reach Mandarin fluency.

In order to apply, students must have 135 hours of Mandarin teaching or equivalent (lower intermediate level), a minimum GPA of 2.5, and be currently enrolled at university or graduated.

Courses offered: Readings in Chinese, Spoken Chinese, Chinese Listening Comprehension, Chinese Language and Culture Practicum, all at intermediate or advanced levels. Additionally, the program organizes trips around Beijing and China several times a year (for example to Xian, Kaifeng, Shanghai)

Cost

Tuition: $27,300 for a full academic year, $14,850 for a single semester. Cost includes housing and program-organized travel and extracurricular activities.

Scholarships: The following companies will sponsor the cost of study at CIEE's Mandarin program: Wollitzer Merit Scholarships in Area or Comparative Studies, Ping Scholarships for Academic Excellence, Global Access Initiative (GAIN) Grants, CIEE Gilman Go Global Grant.

Contact: For more information, refer to CIEE's website at www.ciee.org/study-abroad/china/beijing/intensive-chinese-language

Beijing Language and Culture University

The Beijing Language and Culture University also offers a wide selection of courses, with levels from beginner to advanced

Out of all the programs they have the largest variety of elective courses (more than 20) including: HSK Test Preparation, Business Chinese, Chinese Culture taught in English, Chinese Music, Chinese Calligraphy, Chinese Painting, Taichi, etc.

Cost varies depending upon which program you choose to enroll in. Find out more at admission.blcu.edu.cn/en/cjwt/list.htm

Other Chinese language courses in Beijing

Many universities across the city offer Chinese language courses, but the ones listed above are considered the highest quality and the most prestigious. They are also among the most expensive. If you are on a tight budget, you can look into these cheaper alternatives:

- Beijing Foreign Studies University (BFSU)
- Beijing International Studies University (BISU)
- Beijing Normal University (BNU)
- Beijing University of Chemical Technology (BUCT)
- Capital University of Economics and Business (CUEB)
- Communication University of China (CUC)
- Renmin University

Study Visas

Each of these programs will issue you with an Admission Notification and JW202 form, with which you can apply for a study visa at your local Chinese embassy or consulate.

X1 visa: If you intend to study in China for more than six months, you must apply for the X1 visa. This one is only valid for thirty days upon arrival in China. You will need to go to your program's International Students Division as soon as possible and apply for a Residence Permit in order to obtain legal status.

X2 visa: If your planned time of study in China does not exceed six months, you may apply for the X2 visa. This will remain valid until the end of your program.

Scholarships

The Chinese government offers scholarships to foreign students who wish to study Mandarin at any of the programs listed above. There are two companies where you can apply:

- **Chinese Government Scholarship** www.csc.edu.cn/ Laihua/scholarshipen.aspx
- **Confucius Scholarship** cis.chinese.cn

CHAPTER ELEVEN

How to Transfer Money out of China

✲

Once you are a high-rolling English teacher, you're going to need a way to get your stacks of bills back home. One suitcase might not contain them all, and TSA doesn't take kindly to people traveling with carts full of cash, so what are your other options?

In most countries earning money is the hard part, and getting it home is easy. But China likes to do things differently. The depreciating yuan was causing people to rush to exchange their RMB for dollars, so the Chinese government put restrictions on transferring RMB out the country in order to make things more difficult.

To transfer your money out of China, you have five options:

WESTERN UNION

Western Union is an American company that specializes in wiring money. Because of Chinese laws, you can only send a maximum of $500 at a time through Western Union. If you need to transfer $5,000, you will need to go ten different times.

Important note: Unless you can provide evidence of a legitimate source of income and tax payment, you can only send out $500 from your account per day. So if you're hoping to empty your account of cash, then Western Union/PayPal it home, you will have to plan in advance to give yourself enough time to complete the process.

MAO MONEY MAO PROBLEMS

If you are properly documented in China, you can send home your full legal income, minus tax.

If you are not fully documented (i.e., you are working on a business or tourist visa), the daily limit is $500.

Chinese citizens' international transfers are capped at $2,000 per day and $50,000 per year.

(Un)fortunately most ESL teachers do not need to worry about this, as our salary is unlikely to exceed that amount.

Cost for Western Union Money Wires

- $15 when sending $1-500,
- $20 when sending $501

In most countries you can complete the transfer online, but because of fraud issues in China you are required to physically go to the bank to send money. You will need your passport, a Chinese phone number, and an address.

You will also need to provide the following information for the receiver: full name, passport/ID number, country, address, and phone number.

The following Chinese banks support Western Union, and you can go to any of their branches to complete the transfer:

- Agricultural Bank of China (中国农业银行)

- Bank of Jilin (吉林银行)

- Bank of Wenzhou (温州银行)

- Bank of Yantai (烟台银行)

- Construction Bank of China (receive only) (中国建设银行)

- Everbright Bank of China (中国光大银行)

- Fujian Haixia Bank (福建海峡银行)

- Harbin Bank (哈尔滨银行)

- Huishang Bank (徽商银行)

- Longjiang Bank (龙江银行)

- Postal Saving Bank of China (中国邮政储蓄银行)
- Shanghai Pudong Development Bank (上海浦东发展银行)
- Zhejiang Chouzhou Commercial Bank
  (浙江稠州商业银行)

PAYPAL

Set up a free account on PayPal with your home bank account. Then set up another PayPal account with your Chinese bank account (the PayPal website is in English so this is not difficult.) You will need two bank accounts and two email addresses in order to do this.

You can then transfer your money from your Chinese PayPal to your home PayPal. There is no limit on the amount of money for which you can do this, though you will pay a fee of about $50 for every $500 you send home. So if you're sending back $2,000, you will end up with $1,800.

Some people consider this fee too steep, but this is possibly the most convenient way to send money home.

USE YOUR UNIONPAY CARD ABROAD

If you have a Chinese bank account, you most likely have a UnionPay card to take out money. These cards can be used at ATMs in most Western countries, where you can take out up to 10,000 RMB at a time. You might be charged a $5 fee at the ATM.

Make sure your home country will have ATMs that accept UnionPay—many do, from France to the UK to the US, but not all, so it can't hurt to doublecheck.

BITCOIN

You can buy Bitcoins in China using RMB, then transfer them to a Bitcoin wallet such as quadrigacx. You can then sell the Bitcoin for dollars and withdraw once you are home. The whole process takes thirty minutes to complete and one-two days to clear. This is another way to entirely circumvent money transfer restrictions.

BANK TRANSFER

Chinese banks allow you to transfer up to $500 a day without proof of legal income/tax payments. If you have income and tax payment proof, the limit to how much you can transfer is your full income after tax.

You can also get a Chinese friend to make the transfer for you—Chinese people are allowed to transfer up to $50,000 a year out of China.

To complete the transfer yourself, you will need the following:

1. Your passport (with a valid visa, and bring your residence permit just in case)

2. Employment contract, income proof, and tax receipt with official stamps for every month of your employment

3. SWIFT code for your bank account back home

4. Bank account information for both the sender and the receiver (full name, address, etc.)

Some people are not able to provide the employment contract and tax receipts, either because they are not working legally or because the company is disorganized and has not been paying appropriate taxes. In that case, you will need to take a trusted Chinese friend or colleague to help you with the transfer. You can transfer the necessary amount to his account, and then he will make the transfer abroad. Chinese banks don't really like it when foreigners do this, but you can tell them your friend's son/cousin/long-lost mother has encountered difficulties while traveling abroad and you are trying to help them out.

You will need the following:

1. A Chinese person

2. Your passport (with a valid visa)

3. Chinese person's national identity card

4. SWIFT code for your bank account back home

5. Bank account information for both the sender and the receiver (full name, address, etc.)

ENGLISH BOOKSTORES

Every once in a while I feel guilty at what a philistine Beijing has turned me into and vow to better myself intellectually. Usually a few Tsingtao beers will cure the impulse, but occasionally it gets the best of me and I feel compelled to crack open a book. The question is how to get my hands on some English-language books in China?

Chinese Bookstores

Chinese bookstores don't typically have a foreign-language section. They might have an English section, but this will only offer TOEFL, IELTS, and other study books intended for ESL learners. I love TOEFL as much as the next person (not at all) but test prep books are not the most intellectually stimulating for native English speakers.

Online

Your best bet to find reasonably priced English books is online, either on Taobao or Amazon. Yes, Amazon works in China! Delivery can take up to six weeks, however, which is basically a lifetime. By that point the whim to read will probably be long gone. You will also be paying regular Western prices, which will seem like shameless thievery once you get used to Chinese prices.

If you have AliPay you can use Taobao. Taobao sells everything under the sun, including a decent selection of English language books. The risk when you're buying from Taobao is that you'll end up with a cheap photocopy of a book instead of the real thing,

HONG KONG'S MISSING BOOKSELLERS

In 1997, Hong Kong, once a colony of the United Kingdom, was formally transferred back into the jurisdiction of Beijing.

Traditionally emancipation from a colonial ruler is something to be celebrated, but many Hong Kongers feared they would lose the civil liberties they had enjoyed under British rule. The Chinese government assured them this would not be the case.

Beijing promised Hong Kong that it would be ruled under a policy of "one country, two systems": The city would maintain its capitalist economic and political freedom (including freedom of the press), but would remain an integral part of Chinese territory. The government appeared committed to this policy for more than a decade.

Causeway Bay Books was a notorious Hong Kong bookshop with connections to Mighty Currant, a company that published books on history and politics that were critical of the Chinese Communist Party, controversial biographies of Chinese leaders, and salacious gossip reports about public figures. Causeway Bay Books and Mighty Currant continued to thrive as Hong Kong entered the new millennium.

In 2015, employees of Causeway Bay Books began vanishing mysteriously. By the end of the year, five booksellers were missing without a trace. Family and friends did not hear from them for months. The Chinese government denied any connection to the disappearances.

Gui Minhai appears on TV to confess his sins.

In January 2016, Gui Minhai (a Swedish citizen) appeared on China's national broadcasting channel, CCTV. In a tearful confession, Gui admitted that he had killed a college student in a hit and run eleven years previously, been racked by guilt ever since, and finally decided to turn himself in to the police. All five booksellers eventually revealed guilt to various misdeeds. These admissions are viewed as somewhat fishy due to China's tradition of extracting forced confessions to justify imprisonment of dissidents.

which is fine if you just want something to flip through quickly. But if you like books for decor as well as intellectual enrichment, you'll probably want an authentic copy. In that case, be wary of suspiciously cheap prices—if a book costs 10 RMB it is probably not the real deal.

The best way to be sure of what you're buying is to go directly to an...

English-Language Bookstore

Buying books online is fast and convenient, but I have a soft spot for physical bookstores. I could spend a day wandering around the aisles, flipping through the pages, reading the back covers, catching glimpses of all the hundreds of thousands of stories humans have come up with.

Unfortunately, Beijing does not have great English-language bookstores. If you have obscure tastes (i.e., not world-famous classics and international bestsellers) you'd best stick to Taobao. Additionally, many Western books are banned in China, particularly those relating to Chinese history and politics. If you want a Chinese history book you'll have to go abroad, unless the book is titled Glory to the Communist Party and Everything It Has Ever Done.

Nonetheless, there are a few English-language bookstores to check out. Here are the three largest:

Wangfujing Foreign Language Bookstore

Wangfujing Bookstore is the biggest English bookshop in Beijing. It has a fine selection of classics and the kinds of books that would be assigned in school, but it is lacking in the contemporary

The Bookworm on a cozy November afternoon.

literature and nonfiction departments. Still, if you're looking for a cheap copy of Shakespeare or Jane Austen, you can't go wrong here. Be warned it is quite disorganized—ask the attendant where to find a book and he will join you in wandering futilely around the shop, clearly just as lost as you, until you give up and leave.

Address: 235 Wangfujing Dajie Dongcheng District 东城区 王府井大街235号

Page One

Page One is an international chain, and their Beijing branch is large and organized. They offer a good selection of bestsellers and classics, as well as some heavy coffee table type books. It's the best place to buy contemporary fiction and nonfiction in Beijing. It's located in Sanlitun bar and shopping area, where you'll pay Western prices for a Western environment.

Address: B2/F, China World Summit Wing, 1 Jianguomenwai Dajie Chaoyang District 朝阳区 建国门外大街1号国贸商城三期地下2层

The Bookworm

The Bookworm is not a bookstore in the classic sense of the word—it is more of a cafe/restaurant lined with bookshelves. They specialize in books about China—travel, history, culture, etc. (though again, any book of a politically sensitive nature will not be available). They also have a lending library and used books section. The Bookworm is best known as an intellectual gathering place. It regularly hosts movie screenings, lectures, comedy shows, and publicity events for writers. A pleasant gathering place for the nerds of Beijing. They also have branches in a couple of other major Chinese cities.

Address: Courtyard 4, Gongti Beilu Chaoyang District 朝阳区 工体北路4号院

KTV

The first time a Chinese friend took me to KTV, I was appalled to see there was no alcohol in the room. The idea of spending three hours in an intimate environment singing karaoke, completely sober, was incomprehensible to me. And yet like most foreigners I quickly adapted to the concept, and now we all agree that KTV is one of the great Chinese inventions on par with the compass, paper, and gunpowder.

For those unfamiliar with the concept, KTV is a popular pastime in East Asia that consists of renting a private room with your friends for several hours and singing all your favorite songs on karaoke. KTVs have little shops that offer a wide variety of snacks and alcohol, but alcohol is not a requirement or even expectation of the activity. Public singing is part of the culture, and people here are less self-conscious about their voices than Westerners. Any village worthy of the name will have at least one KTV, and traditional Chinese who wouldn't dream of going to a nightclub will spend the midnight hours singing their hearts out instead.

KTV's role as China's go-to nighttime entertainment has given it a salacious reputation—"KTV girls" is a euphemism for prostitutes, and in cities with a drug epidemic, KTVs' notoriety as dens of debauchery have made them the targets of police raids. But for most people, KTVs are simply an alternative to clubs, with the additional assurance that the music and the company will be good since you get to choose both.

PUTTING THE K IN KTV

Ketamine, also known as K, is a horse tranquilizer and the fastest-growing recreational drug in the world. Currently its largest market is the Middle Kingdom.

Two big K busts brought the drug to public attention in the past 10 years. Both took place in KTVs.

One thousand people were arrested in a KTV in Dongguan, Guangdong province in 2013. There was evidence of K consumption in 57 of the KTV rooms.

The second bust was smaller in scale but larger in scandal: In 2015 a group of bourgeois housewives in Wenzhou, Zhejiang province, were arrested during a night out at a KTV. Of the twenty arrested, sixteen were women in their forties to fifties, and all tested positive for Ketamine.

Gives a whole new meaning to Desperate Housewives.

CHAPTER TWELVE
Overview of Religion in China

A 2015 survey by Gallup International and WI Network found that China is the most atheistic country in the world, with ninety percent of respondents saying they identified as atheist or not religious. This should not shock anyone who knows the relationship between communism and religion—the former sees the latter as a method of oppressing the proletariat. Chairman Mao sought to eradicate the influence of religion in China throughout his nearly thirty years in power. This in conjunction with a lack of history of dominant monotheistic, organized religions such as Christianity, Judaism, and Islam has resulted in a country of non-believers.

China does have a heritage of Buddhism and other Eastern religions like Taoism and Confucianism. Chinese cities and countryside are dotted with temples, and a visit to any of these will reveal the tradition of lighting incense and prostrating to Buddhist statues is alive and well. The Lama Temple of Beijing is still active with monks who tend the grounds and preserve their legacy. The Chinese government is willing to accept moderate Buddhism until sects grow large and powerful enough to be seen as a threat to its authority — see China's persecution of Tibetan Buddhism and the Falun Gong.

There are some religious strongholds that are resisting attempts at eradication. Fifty-eight percent of the inhabitants of Xinjiang Province, in the northwest of China, are practicing Muslims. These Muslims are mostly of the Uyghur and Hui ethnic minorities, with ethnic, cultural, and linguistic roots to Turkey. The Uyghurs have engendered a separatist movement that believes China illegally annexed Xinjiang in 1949, and since then the province has been the site of violent demonstrations and clashes between Chinese police and separatist movements. Religion and politics are deeply intertwined in Xinjiang — the government hopes that by stifling religion it can make the Uyghurs conform with the rest of the country. Hence a string of anti-religion laws passed in the region — for example, a 2014 ban for civil servants from fasting during Ramadan, or a 2015 decree forcing shops to sell alcohol despite the fact it is against the Muslim faith.

Despite the government's best efforts, religion has proved hard to contain. Christianity in particular has been growing in size and influence. Earliest indications of Christian faith in China appears in writings from 700 AD, and Western missionaries sought to expand their faith in China after the early 1800s. The Christian faith grew until the Communists took power and forbade religious activities. Since the 1970s, restrictions have eased, and now official government statistics show that there are approximately 26 million Christians registered in China. Yet international Christian organizations suspect there are tens of millions more unregistered Christians who practice their faith in underground churches and congregations.

RELIGION FOR FOREIGNERS

The official stance the Chinese government is that although foreigners are allowed to worship while in China, they are forbidden from proselytizing and spreading their religion. Members of the Mormon community have told me that they can maintain an active Church but they are forbidden from discussing their faith with Chinese people. Members of the Jewish community in Beijing admitted to having illicit temples disguised as kosher restaurants in order to circumvent restrictions on number of temples in Beijing. But overall during my time in Beijing I have met a wide variety of foreigners of different religions, and none felt that they were restricted in their ability to practice their faith while in China.

Are you religious? Here are some organizations that will keep you in touch with your faith in Beijing.

CHRISTIAN

Beijing International Christian Fellowship (BICF)

BICF is a non-denominational Christian organization that offers sermons in nine languages (English, Korean, Japanese, Indonesian, French, and Mandarin among them). It also offers bible study groups, catechisms, and cultural activities for Christians in Beijing. They have multiple addresses and worship groups around the city, so you can find one conveniently located near you.

Website: www.bicf.org

Headquarters: 朝阳区　亮马桥路40号21世纪饭店2层FA201室 Rm FA201, 2/F, 21st Century Hotel, 40 Liangmaqiao Lu Chaoyang District

Beijing Baptist Church

The Beijing Baptist Church offers English-language sermons every Sunday at 10 A.M. at the German Center near Liangmaqiao subway station.

Website: www.beijingbaptistchurch.org

Address: 朝阳区, 北京市, 东方东路19号, D号楼, 11层, 1101室.

JEWISH

Note: Because Judaism is not an officially recognized religion in China, the government requires that Jewish events be open only to foreign passport-holders. Mainland Chinese citizens will be turned away from the following organizations.

Kehillat Beijing

The Kehillat was the first Jewish organization established in Beijing, in 1979. It offers Shabat services every Friday at 7 P.M., as well as a wide selection of Jewish educational, cultural, and religious services. The Kehillat serves liberal and reformed Jews.

Website: www.sinogogue.org

Address: 中国北京朝阳区新源南路6号京城大厦旁边的京城俱乐部3层Capital Club Athletic Center 3rd Floor Ballroom Capital Mansion, 6 Xinyuan Nanlu Chaoyang District, Beijing

Chabad Beijing:

The Chabad Beijing was established in 2001 in response to the growing needs of Beijing's expanding Jewish population. It also strives to cater to Beijing's transitive Jews—tourists and businessmen here on a temporary basis. The Chabad focuses on Jewish educational and cultural enrichment classes, as well as Shabat services. It directs Northern China's only Jewish day school.

Website: www.chabadbeijing.com

Address: 芳园西路，四得公园南门旁 Fang Yuan Xi Lu, next to the south gate of Si De Park

ISLAMIC

Islam has a long history in China, and currently there are an estimated 23 million Muslims in the country, mostly concentrated in the Western provinces. Beijing has a large Islamic community as well—around 250,000 practicing Muslims, mostly of the Hui minority. There are hundreds of halal restaurants and shops across the city, and plenty of mosques that offer worship services. This doesn't include the large community of Muslim foreigners living and working in Beijing—Pakistanis, Iranians, and Indians among them.

Highlights

Niu Jie Mosque (牛街清真寺)
Built in 996 AD, Nuijie Mosque is one of the oldest mosques in China. The mosque is built in the Muslim enclave of Beijing in the Southwest of the city, where Hui men and women in traditional caps and headscarves wander around the street's halal and Arabian shops and restaurants. Niu Jie Mosque caters mostly to the local Hui population, but

Built in 996 AD, Beijing's Niujie Mosque in Beijing is one of the oldest in China.

any Muslim is free to enter and participate in its religious services. Any non-Muslim should also go take a look, as the mosque is a fascinating blend of Chinese and Arabian style architecture and decoration.

Address: 西城区牛街18号, in Xuanwu district of Beijing.

Dongsi Mosque (东四清真寺)
Dongsi Mosque is the second-largest Mosque in Beijing after Niu Jie. It is the home of the Islamic Association of China, which researches Islamic history in China and organizes

cultural and educational activities. Dongsi Mosque is welcoming to foreign Muslims living in and traveling through Beijing, and offers prayer services five times a day.

Address: 北京市东城区东四南大街13号13 Dongsi Nanda Jie, Dongcheng District

IN THE MOOD FOR LOVE

Unless you are married or a monk, you will probably end up having some experience with dating life in China.

If you are a man, the good news is that the dating market will be very favorable to you—in China the stereotype that Westerners are all rich persists, which makes foreign men desirable to women. A Western boyfriend is a nice trophy and status symbol for Chinese women. Male expats report that living in China is a refreshing experience because it is the first time they get to experience being pursued by women instead of having to do all the chasing. So men can sit back and enjoy the attention.

But Westerners need to be aware of different cultural expectations of dating—Chinese people take relationships seriously, and most don't do casual sex. This doesn't mean that women will refuse to sleep with you—just that the act will hold significant importance in their eyes. Tales of hapless foreigners who have a one-night stand with a Chinese girl, then are surprised when the next morning they learn that she now believes they are in a committed relationship and reacts badly to being told otherwise, abound in China.

"I'd rather cry in the back of a BMW than laugh on the back of a bicycle."

— Quote from a Chinese dating show

Typical conversation the author has had with Chinese men on many occasions:

Man: Oh, you are American?

Sophia: Yes.

Man: That's great. American women are not shy.

Sophia: Hmm.

Man: I've heard Americans are very open. Is that true?

Sophia [in her head]: What does that mean, "Americans are very open"? Open what? Open mind, open heart, open wallet? There are 360 million Americans with a wide variety of personalities, characteristics, attitudes, and beliefs. How do I respond to a question like that?

Sophia [out loud]: I guess.

Man: Will you have sex with me?

Sophia: No.

Couples composed of a foreign man and a Chinese woman are an ordinary sight across China, but the opposite is not nearly as common. Chinese men seem to be shy of approaching Western women, though sometimes they will tentatively say they've heard foreign girls are very "open" (i.e. slutty) and ask if you want to have sex. Again, cultural misunderstandings can cause trouble in relationships—Chinese couples tend to hold more traditional gender roles where the woman cooks and cleans and doesn't go out at night, and the man must pay for dates and gifts for the girl. This gendered dynamic can be frustrating for liberated Western women.

Despite these challenges, there are plenty of examples of successful cross-cultural partnerships. If you are up for the challenge, you can turn to dating apps to find your own Chinese soul mate. The most commonly used are:

- **Tantan:** A shameless rip-off of Tinder, except Tinder is banned in China
- **WeChat People Nearby:** WeChat offers a service that lets you connect to other people nearby who are using WeChat (i.e., everyone). Although People Nearby is not officially a dating service, that seems to be its most common usage.
- **Tinder:** Despite the fact Tinder is banned, many expats still use it. The advantage of using Tinder over Tantan is that since you need a VPN to access the app it tends to attract Chinese people who speak English and have some experience of the Western world. There is therefore less of a cultural divide to bridge. Tinder is also the favorite dating app of expat men and women, so a good way for us to meet each other.

SORRY, WESTERN GIRLS
ARE NOT THAT OPEN

A couple of years ago I dated a Chinese guy for a few months. I met him on a dating app, which he told me he used specifically to find foreign girls. He frequently made comments about how he preferred Western girls because they were more "open" and he thought Chinese girls were too conservative and traditional. All his exes were also Westerners.

We'd started sleeping together and had been going on more and more dates. One night he invited me over to his place saying he wanted to introduce me to a friend of his. I went, thinking this was an indication that things were getting more serious between us, because I hadn't met any of his friends before.

When I arrived, I noticed that there were several unopened bottles of whiskey and coke on the table, which was strange because I had never seen him drink anything more than a can of beer with dinner.

He introduced me to his friend, and immediately they asked if I wanted to take a shot. We had a few drinks before he held up his phone dramatically and said he had to leave immediately because a friend of his was sick and he needed to take him to the hospital. I stood up to leave but he insisted we should both stay without him as long as we wanted, and told us to have fun.

After he left, his friend started plying me with whiskey, asking about my past sexual experiences and what I thought about Chinese boys. When I wouldn't drink more he asked me what was my favorite kind of alcohol, then said he was going to go downstairs to buy it. It was getting uncomfortable so I left. He escorted me to the door with a disappointed look.

"I really hoped you would spend the night with me," he said. I laughed awkwardly and hurried away.

The next day my boyfriend texted as if nothing was wrong. I ignored him for a few days until he asked me if I was angry at him for some reason.

"Did you make up an excuse to leave me with your friend last weekend so we would sleep together?" I texted him.

"Yeah he saw ur picture and thought u were cute and asked me to help him spend the night with u"

"I'm not a prostitute you can share with your friends."

(continued)

"I'm sorry u feel that way. That's not what I meant at all. I thought western girls were open about this kind of thing. Didn't u like him?"

I didn't dignify that with a response. He tried messaging me a few more times, finally to ask me if I had any pretty friends to set him up with.

After that I blocked him.

LGBT LIFE

The twenty-first century has witnessed a transformation in gay rights. While twenty years ago no major political figure would openly endorse gay marriage, a swift tide of public opinion has led to gay partnerships being recognized across most liberal democracies. In many circles of the Western world, it has become more shocking to say you oppose gay rights than the contrary.

NO HOMO

When I came to China I was surprised to see many young women openly walking around holding hands. "What a progressive, forward-thinking country," I thought, before learning that holding hands in China is a common platonic gesture, and these women would be appalled to hear how it could be interpreted by a foreigner.

Likewise for young men massaging each other's shoulders and thighs in class—just friends. There's no faster way to make a class of young men break out into hysterical laughter than make the preposterous suggestion that one of them might be gay. Amusement for days.

The reverberations of this revolution have reached all the way to China. A country of 1.4 billion people is bound to have a few homosexuals, and as the world has proved it is possible for societies to accept different sexual orientations, Chinese gays have become more willing to expose themselves.

In 2015, a gay man proposed to his boyfriend on a crowded Beijing subway. "I want everyone I know or I don't know to witness this. I will be loving you for the rest of my life," the man says, while the crowd watches in smiling bemusement, eventually cheering as the two embrace. The video went viral in China, shared more than 10,000 times on Sina Weibo (China's equivalent to Twitter).

Reactions are not always so supportive, however. Another notorious case involved a lesbian proposing to her girlfriend during their 2016 graduation ceremony from Guangdong University of Foreign Studies. The video also went viral on Weibo, before being deleted by censors. Within the next few days, several Weibo accounts related to gender and sexuality were also deleted. The girl who proposed was threatened with disciplinary action by the university's Communist Party committee, and her graduation certificate was withheld.

Although anecdotal evidence suggests that attitudes towards gays and lesbians are shifting among young, urban demographics, social progress is slow. Many Chinese view the rise of LGBT communities in China as yet another example of corrupting influence from the West.

LGBT acceptance faces a unique challenge in China. Because of the one-child policy, parents fear having a gay child means they

THE ROSETTA STONE:
CHINGLISH EDITION

Comrade: 同志(pinyin: tóngzhì, slang term for gay man)

This slang term for gay supposedly became popular during the Cultural Revolution, when the Communist Party cracked down on homosexuality as a counter-revolutionary practice. A middle finger to the CCP, if you will.

E.g. "Hey comrade, is your name Karl Marx? 'Cause you're starting an uprising in my lower classes ;) "

will have no heirs to carry on the bloodline. Though the one-child policy officially came to an end in 2015, the birth rate is stubbornly refusing to rise. For now, gay Chinese continue to face intense pressure from their parents to marry and provide them with a grandchild. This has led to the rise of convenience marriage apps, which partner up lesbian couples with gay couples so they can enter into a marriage contract and appease their families while staying true to their sexual orientation. ChinaGayles.com is the most popular such dating site, and has matched more than 23,000 couples since it was started in 2005.

The silver lining is that homophobia in China rarely manifests itself in violence. While gay Chinese are discriminated against in the workplace, gay foreigners are accepted under the blanket justification that "foreigners are different." Gay expats can easily meet through dating apps like Grindr and Tinder, and there is a thriving LGBT scene in all the major cities of China. There is no reason to let fear of intolerant attitudes keep you away.

LGBT ORGANIZATIONS IN BEIJING

Beijing LGBT Center (北京同志中心)

The Beijing LGBT centers seeks to promote LGBT interests, eliminate discrimination, and improve the life of China's LGBT community.

Address: 朝阳区 北京市朝阳区西坝河南路甲1号新天第大厦 B座2606室

GAY AND LESBIAN BARS

Adam's

A laid-back, low-key bar in the center of Sanlitun district. Proudly flies a rainbow flag.

Address: 40 Sanlitun lu, Chaoyang district, 朝阳区三里屯路40号

Destination

Biggest gay club in Beijing, overflowing with drunken expats on a Friday or Saturday night. Cheap drinks and good location in the middle of Sanlitun Bar Street.

WILL CHINA'S HOMOPHOBIA HAVE AN IMPACT ON HOLLYWOOD?

In 2016, the Chinese government issued a new guideline stating that movies and TV shows "exaggerating the dark side of society" could no longer be released in China.

"The dark side of society" includes "abnormal sexual relationships and behaviors, such as incest, same-sex relationships, sexual perversion, sexual assault, sexual abuse, sexual violence, and so on." A popular TV show, which followed the relationship of two gay men, was then pulled off the internet.

This law could have repercussions for Hollywood. The restrictive yet enormously lucrative Chinese market is the El Dorado of the film industry. Producers court it by including Chinese settings, characters, and actors in blockbuster releases.

LGBT activists are concerned that producers will restrict themselves in accordance with Chinese morality laws in order to maintain access to the Mainland. This would limit the ability of Hollywood producers to portray LGBT actors in big blockbuster movies.

Address: 7 Gongti Xilu Chaoyang District 朝阳区 工体西路7号

Les Booze

Les Booze is lesbian night at Chill Cafe on the first Friday and third Saturday of every month. Enjoy the courtyard setting and cheap beers as well as karaoke and open mic night.

Address: 2 Andingmen Xidajie (50m west from southwest corner of Andingmen Qiao) Dongcheng District 东城区 安定门西大街2号 （安定门桥西南边往西走50米）

明

View from my office, on a clear and smoggy day

CHAPTER THIRTEEN
Pollution (and Other Hazards)

A guide to China cannot be complete without some warning about the country's infamous smog. No doubt you've seen the pictures in the media — buildings shrouded in an opaque haze, phantom figures walking in the mist with their faces hidden by bulky breathing masks. From the pieces that regularly run in the Western media you would believe China is two factories away from suffocating its 1.4 billion citizens.

The media has overblown the issue of smog in China, but there is no denying haze and pollution will be a fact of life here. The extent to which it will affect you depends on your location — Beijing and the whole northeast section of the country are traditionally hit the hardest due to an unfortunate combination of geographic and economic factors.

If you have sensitive lungs or are concerned about long-term damage to your health, your best bet will be to move southeast. Shenzhen, Kunming, Haikou, Xiamen, Huizhou, Zhongshan, Zhuhai, and Fuzhou are the only eight cities in China to regularly meet the World Health Organization's standards for safe levels of air pollution. They're also very livable: Shenzhen and Kunming are both highly developed Tier 2 cities with plenty of opportunities for foreigners. Haikou and Xiamen are coastal towns that attract millions of tourists each year with their sunny beaches and lush nature.

But those cities are the exception, not the rule. You will experience smog in almost any large city in China. If you are willing to accept pollution as an unfortunate byproduct of life in the Middle Kingdom, here's what you need to know:

What is the AQI?

AQI stands for Air Quality Index. The AQI is determined by measuring the concentration of five different polluting particles in the air: ground-level ozone, particle pollution, carbon monoxide, sulfur dioxide, and nitrogen dioxide. These particles cause damage to our bodies by infiltrating our lungs and our bloodstream.

In Beijing, the Chinese government and the American embassy measure the concentration of these fine particles in the air and release a rating every hour or so. This rating is the **AQI**, and it is usually a number between 0 and 500. It is based on the concentration of pollutants in the air. An AQI number below 100 is considered acceptable, and a number higher than 300 is considered hazardous to human health.

There are many apps that will keep you informed of the latest AQI, and most Chinese phones have an air pollution index built in with the weather widget.

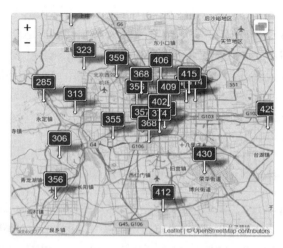

AQI map on a typical winter day in Beijing. Just a tad higher than the WHO recommended limit of 25.

The World Health Organization advises that an AQI of 25 is the highest pollution humans can safely breathe long-term. All but the eight cities mentioned above regularly exceed that level, and nation-wide the average pollution index is closer to 80. The WHO and the International Agency for Research on Cancer have classified air pollution as a Class 1 carcinogen, which puts it on an equal footing with tobacco. Long-term exposure to polluting air molecules has been linked to heart disease and a whole gamut of unpleasant respiratory illnesses. On average, regular exposure to air pollution shortens one's lifespan by about three years.

These are grim statistics, but bear in mind that they apply to those who have been exposed to these particles for their entire lifetime. A year or two in Beijing in unlikely to have a severe detrimental effect on your health—unless you already suffer from asthma and other pre-existing conditions, in which case you need to consult with your doctor before making the move.

Air Pollution Apps to Download

- **China Air Quality Index:** Offers air quality updates for more than 240 cities in China. The app takes info from up to thirty monitoring stations in each city so you can avoid the particularly smoggy neighborhoods. Free

- **Wake Me Run Run**: This app allows you to set an alarm dependent on the air quality in the morning. If you're a jogger who prefers morning runs, you can set the alarm to wake you up only if the pollution levels are classified as healthy—so you don't wake up for no reason. $1.99

- **Airpocalypse**: China's pollution can get us all a little down sometimes. This app injects some black humor to cheer us up on those gray days. It gives you a clever one-liner with each AQI reading—for example, AQI 360 is "Baijiu for your lungs!" You will almost find yourself wishing the AQI would keep rising to see what joke the app will come up with next. Free

HOW TO PROTECT YOURSELF

The good news is that you are not totally at the mercy of the fearsome PM 2.5 gods. There are two ways to protect your lungs: mouth masks and air purifiers.

Mouth masks

You've probably seen pictures of Chinese walking around with what looks like surgeon masks on their faces. While those might have their use in an operating room, they are a poor defense against the smog. All but the biggest pollution particles can be breathed in through the thin fabric.

Mouth mask technology has evolved to adapt to the times, and the latest rage in Beijing is the 3M variant. These are thick, bulky and undeniably ugly, but they can protect you against the worst of the pollution. You have to make sure the mask molds tightly to your face, otherwise air will squeeze in through the sides instead of through the ventilator. The ventilator is the mechanism through which harmful air particles are filtered out. They can be bought in any corner shop in China for RMB 5-9 ($0.74-1.35). Generally they will last up to a week in heavy pollution. When the masks blacken and the ventilator clogs with grime, you'll know it's time to get a new one.

Unfortunately, the fact that mouth masks wouldn't look out of place in a dystopian thriller means they are not the most stylish accessory in the world, but some Chinese fashionistas have tried to revamp their image. If you don't generally go for the "survivor of the nuclear Apocalypse" look, you can try out the cutesy masks instead.

Just make sure they have an air ventilator. That is how you distinguish the real masks from the decorative ones.

How Will the Pollution Affect Me in the Short Term?

Most days it won't affect you at all, especially in the summer. May-August rarely exceeds the Unhealthy level. Winters are when the worst of the smog hits as many people still heat up their houses with coal. The dreaded Airpocalypse comes during the deepest winter months, when the index will sky-rocket up to 500 or even 900. Schools will be closed and the entire city will disappear outside the window.

AQI CLASSIFICATION

The Chinese government has six categories for classifying air pollution:

- Good (0-50)
- Moderate (51-100)
- Unhealthy for Sensitive Groups (101-150)
- Unhealthy (151-200)
- Very Unhealthy (201-300)
- Hazardous (300+)

THE ROSETTA STONE
CHINGLISH EDITION

Airpocalypse (portmanteau of air and apocalypse)

When PM 2.5 levels are so high you can feel yourself developing lung cancer (500+)

E.g. It's the Airpocalypse today and the haze is so thick I can't see my feet.

Most people don't physically feel the effect of air pollution until it reaches Hazardous status. At 400, your nose will start running with black mucus, you throat will itch, your cotton swabs will come out of your ears coated in grime, and you might feel a shortness of breath if you try exercising (not advisable under conditions of heavy pollution—you'll have a good excuse to skip the gym!). You'll need to wash your hair more often and you might notice your coat turning a little gray. Days like this are a good time to Netflix & chill.

Let me stress that it is rare for air pollution to reach Hazardous status—according to the U.S. State Department this occurred less than five percent of the time in the period 2008-2014. Unfortunately, the same survey showed that the air is Unhealthy or worse about eighty percent of the time. Which is why if you move to China you will want to invest in an...

Air Purifier

Many people, Chinese and expats alike, make the mistake of assuming that air pollution is an outside problem, and once inside you are safe. Absolutely incorrect. A 2015 investigation by Chinese real estate agency JLL found that in ninety percent of homes and offices, the concentration of PM 2.5 is equal to or higher than outdoors. The particles sneak in through doors and windows and then get trapped without any wind to blow them away.

So should you start wearing your mask all the time? If you don't care about talking and breathing comfortably that is certainly one solution. If you do value those activities, I recommend outfitting your apartment with an air purifier.

Air purifiers can range in price from RMB 300 to 10,000 ($45-1,500). Many consumers have an innate suspicion of the cheaper options, but as long as the purifier has been certified with a High-Efficiency Particle Arrestance (HEPA) filter it will be able to eliminate eighty-five to almost one hundred percent of the unhealthy air particles.

The basic model

All air purifiers, even the ones that bill themselves as high-end technology, are essentially a fan plus a filter. If you are the DIY type you can buy these two components by yourself and attach the filter to the fan, and place it in a corner of your room. A HEPA filter can be bought at Best Buy, Home Depot, Walmart, or any supermarket in China. The price should not exceed RMB 100 ($15).

How to do it: Buy a basic twenty-inch by twenty-inch fan and a HEPA-certified filter (should be around $15). Then simply tape the filter over the fan (make sure the arrows are facing out) and you're done!

Air Purifying Machines

If you prefer to play it safe with a store-bought air purifier, here are your options:

Mid-range:

Chinese brands Yadu and Midea offer air purifiers with prices ranging from RMB 800 to 10,000 ($120-1,500). For the same price you can also find options by foreign brands like Panasonic, Philips, and Sharp. These can be found in any mall or supermarket in China.

High-End

The most high-tech air purifiers are made by Blueair, IQAir, and Alen for prices exceeding RMB 10,000 ($1,500). These are targeted to people suffering from strong allergies, asthma, and other respiratory illnesses, and filter out germs and bacteria as well PM 2.5 particles. If the only reason you are buying an air purifier is to protect against pollution, these high-end brands are probably not worth the cost.

Air purifiers are generally not very large, about twenty-inch by twenty-inch. They are designed to clean a single room, not a whole apartment. Place one in the corner of the rooms where you spend the most time. Keep it away from windows and doors so the machine doesn't clean air that is heading out anyway—you want it focused on the stale air inside.

Whichever model you buy, **make sure it has a HEPA certification**. Otherwise, you're just buying a glorified fan. And remember to replace the filter whenever it starts to clog with particles and turn black (how fast this happens depends on the level of pollution—on bad days try to change it every day), otherwise the filter becomes useless.

If you wear your mask and run an air purifier, you should be protected from the most severe effects of the smog. Don't get complacent, however—there are still plenty of other hazards to threaten your health in China.

FAKE FOOD

One term you will often hear in China is "fake food," and no, that doesn't refer to GMOs or artificial flavoring. Examples of fake food in China run more along the lines of rice made of plastic, dumplings stuffed with cardboard, and empty egg shells filled with cheap chemicals.

Are plastic, cardboard, and chemicals obscure Chinese delicacies? No. These products are a way for vendors to skim off a couple kuai from the manufacturing process, at the expense of customers' health.

BABY FORMULA SCANDAL

One particular incident brought China's fake food industry to the attention of the international press: the 2008 fake baby formula scandal.

After dozens of babies in Gansu province were mysteriously diagnosed with kidney stones, an investigation found that Sanlu, the leading regional manufacturer of baby formula, was adulterating its product with melanin to give it an artificially high protein count. Babies fed on the formula ended up with severe protein deficiencies.

This ultimately caused the deaths of sixteen infants. Another 54,000 were hospitalized for kidney damage, and the government estimates that up to 300,000 babies in total were affected.

Most Egregious Fake Food Scandal

In 2012, a woman in Henan province cracked open her freshly bought eggs and found that they contained a mixture of resin, starch, coagulant and pigments instead of the expected egg whites and yolk. Resin is a favorite among fake food chefs—last year residents in Shaanxi were surprised when their store-bought rice produced a film of plastic in the pan and came out hard and difficult to digest. Turns out it was not rice, but a combination of potatoes and synthetic resin. In 2013 the Global Times (China's government-sanctioned newspaper) arrested more than 900 people involved in a half-decade scam selling fox, mink, and rat meat as mutton to stores and restaurants in Shanghai and Wuxi.

THE ROSETTA STONE: CHINGLISH EDITION

Baijiu (白酒; pinyin: báijiǔ; lit: white alcohol)

Baijiu is China's national drink. It is a hard liquor—between forty and sixty percent alcohol—and is made from grain, usually sorghum or rice.

Baijiu is characterized not by its components but by the distillery process through which it is made. Basically any clear alcohol made in China is called baijiu, and taste varies widely (it is as if gin and vodka and rum all went by "clear booze").

Most foreigners find baijiu revolting, though its cheap price and ubiquitousness mean we often resort to drinking it anyway.

E.g. "Did someone mistakenly pour gasoline in my glass? Oh, wait, that's just baijiu."

It seems every month in China there is some fresh scandal to make you question the origins of the meat on the delicious barbecue sticks ubiquitously sold on the street. Speaking of street food, you should think twice before buying from those little stands selling fried pancakes and noodles whose oily fragrance perfume the night air. **"Gutter oil"** is a term that was coined in 2000 to describe waste oil collected from sewer drains, grease traps, and restaurant fryers and resold as a cheap alternative to cooking oil. Exact statistics on the prevalence of this practice are hard to find, but anecdotal evidence strongly suggests these food stands will cost even the most hardened China veterans a night on the toilet.

What can you do to avoid unsafe foods? Not much, unfortunately. Some people suggest avoiding cheap mom-and-pop eateries in favor of more reputable restaurant chains, but to follow this advice would mean missing out on a huge part of the gastronomic experience of living in China. Just make sure to pack your diarrhea medicine, and if you find the rice in your plate is covered in a film of plastic, for God's sake please don't eat it.

FAKE ALCOHOL

Thought we were done with fake consumables? Think again. As China's bar and drinking industry has skyrocketed in the past decade, it has created a huge underground industry of fake alcohol production.

What is fake alcohol? There are two kinds—the first is inexpensive but still legal booze rebranded as high-end alcohol. The other is unregulated, illegally-produced liquor sold in branded bottles.

The second kind is the most dangerous. Investigations found that unregulated liquor contained high amounts of ethylene glycol (commonly known as antifreeze), methanol (which has been known to cause blindness), and isopropyl alcohol (which is not created for human consumption). When expats gather around the bonfire at night to tell scary tales, they skip the ghost stories in favor of recounting the experiences of friends fainting after a couple of drinks and waking up in a hospital, blind.

The first kind is far more common. Fake alcohol producers will steal or forge international brand bottles (Smirnoff, Jim Beam, etc.) and fill them with cheap, locally-produced alcohol. For example, a 2012 police raid in Guangdong arrested a gang that had been refilling high-end whiskey bottles with 30 RMB a bottle liquor. This practice is often done under highly unhygienic conditions without any government supervision or regulation.

How much alcohol in China is fake? Again, it's hard to find exact statistics. Brown-Forman (the company that produces Jack Daniels) estimates that fake alcohol makes up thirty percent of Chinese liquor sales. The World Health Organizations has issued warnings about the danger of this practice, but so far government attempts to crack down on the industry have shown limited results.

The Hangover's *fourth and final installment,* Blinded in Beijing

Fortunately, there are measures you can take to protect yourself. Bars and nightclubs are the biggest culprits of selling fake alcohol — if your neighborhood dive regularly offers all-night-long free alcohol, you should ask yourself how they can afford to do so. In general, if you are going to bars, stick to bottled beer and wine. If you want hard liquor, find an import shop (Liquor Easy and Cheers are two big chains in China) and buy an entire bottle from them.

DEATH BY BAIJIU

Like most aspects of China, Chinese drinking culture differs from the West. Baijiu is rarely drunk by itself—it is served with a meal. Everyone is given a tiny shot glass. Any time you want to drink you must make a toast, either to the whole group or to a particular person. Then everyone clinks glasses and drinks together. It is impolite to refuse a toast, and men are pressured to drink huge quantities. Having a high alcohol tolerance is vital to success in Chinese business and politics, since deals are made during dinners where baijiu is served.

This practice has its critics. The issue of China's drinking culture was brought under national scrutiny following the death of police officer Chen Lusheng. Chen died in 2010 at a police banquet in Shenzhen, where he choked on his own vomit after overindulging in baijiu. His superiors ruled that his death was "in the line of duty"; this was a professional banquet, and he had no choice but to accept toast after toast until he passed out.

He is not the first Chinese to die in an official capacity, and he won't be the last. It is disrespectful to refuse a toast, and it is also disrespectful not to make toasts at every opportunity, so that leaves Chinese professionals in a Catch-22. Death By Baijiu shall remain in China's future for now.

FIVE WAYS YOU CAN RUIN YOUR EXPERIENCE IN CHINA

1. Working on a tourist visa and getting deported and blacklisted from the country.
2. Getting seriously ill without health insurance.
3. Being too outspoken about Chinese politics on a public platform.
4. Getting wasted on fake alcohol and suffering serious health consequences.
5. Taking drugs and getting thrown in jail for years.

CHAPTER FOURTEEN

Travel in China

One of the major appeals of China is that it is an excellent base for the intrepid traveler. As the Chinese will proudly tell you at every opportunity, China has 5,000 years of history. The country is filled with wonders both natural and man-made, from the vast deserts of Xinjiang to a 233-foot tall Buddha carved in the Sichuan mountains. It's also ideally located to hop on a cheap flight for a weekend trip to Japan, Korea, or around Southeast Asia. It would be a criminal waste to neglect to take advantage of your time here to explore this naturally, culturally, and historically abundant continent. Here's what you need to know about traveling in China.

A NOTE ON HOLIDAYS

If you follow a regular working schedule in China, national holidays might be the only time you have to travel. Be aware that traveling during national holidays can be madness. Never forget that China is a country of 1.4 billion citizens — you don't know the meaning of crowded until you move here.

MYTHBUSTERS: CHINA EDITION

Does China have 5000 years of history?

This is a myth.

Historians mark the beginning of history as the earliest remains of written language. If you count the start of history as the earliest signs of human activity, you could say North America has 13,000 years of history. This would make China's boast meaningless.

While China does have archaeological treasures from 5,000 years ago, its earliest evidence of written language dates from approximately 1000 BC. Yet the idea of 5,000 years of history is such an integral part of China's cultural identity that you will be hard-pressed to find anyone who can be convinced otherwise.

This is especially true of Spring Festival, also known as the world's largest annual human migration. Up to 3 billion trips are taken between January and March each year as migrant workers and city-dwellers return to their ancestral homes for a holiday feast. If you dare to brave the mob during this time, you will have to buy your tickets months in advance. Railway companies will announce when they plan to start ticket sales for particularly crowded journeys, and people will stay up until midnight to get a chance to buy a ticket home. They are often sold out within minutes, and then a black market opens where people resell tickets at exorbitant prices.

Spring Festival is an exceptionally difficult time to travel, as almost all Chinese feel obligated to return to their families during this time. Other holidays are more manageable, but you should still expect large crowds and inflated prices. It's a good idea to plan your trips months in advance to avoid paying extravagant prices or worse, miss the chance to travel at all because tickets are sold out.

DOMESTIC TRAVEL

Train

By far the most popular method of travel in China is train. China has 121,000 kilometers of railways that stretch through the country's mountains, rice paddies, deserts and forests, giving passengers a flashing glimpse into the country's rural scenes. It's worth taking a long train journey at least once while you're here, both to enjoy the views and to appreciate the sophistication of China's rail industry.

There are two kinds of trains: bullet and regular. Both are safe and reliable—unlike flights, trains in China are rarely delayed or cancelled.

THE ROSETTA STONE
CHINGLISH EDITION

Spring Festival (春节, pinyin: chūnjié)

This national holiday marks the beginning of the year according to the Chinese Lunar Calendar. In other words, Spring Festival is what Westerners call Chinese New Year.

Chinese celebrations of Spring Festival mainly involve feasting, setting off enough firecrackers to simulate the effect of a small nuclear bomb, and feasting more.

E.g. "I'm going to stay in my room until Spring Festival ends so I don't get my head blown off by firecrackers."

Bullet trains are identifiable by their smooth, pointed appearance (they are said to look like bullets, hence the name). They are more modern and have better facilities than regular trains (e.g., no squat toilets), making them the first choice for most passengers. There are four types of seat classes offered on a bullet train: first class, second class, business class, and VIP. There are few overnight bullet train journeys, but those that exist also offer soft sleeper, hard sleeper, and luxury sleeper.

Regular trains are slower (obviously) and more chaotic—they are the cheapest option so they attract the poorest Chinese. This is the only kind of train that offers standing tickets and allows people to smoke, so they tend to be crowded and dirty. They offer hard seat, soft seat, and standing tickets.

Ticket Types

Seat classes

For bullet trains:

- **First class:** Four seats in a row, two on each side of the cabin. You get a footrest and the seats are wider than in second class, but other than that there is not much difference.

- **Second class:** These look like the economy class of an airplane. There are five seats in one row, three on one side and two on the other. These seats can be lightly reclined and there is a foldable table in front of you.

- **Business class:** These are only available on a few G and D journeys. If you've ever traveled business class in an airplane the seats will look familiar; they can be reclined all the way until they are almost flat. There are three seats per row: two on one side and one on the other.

- **VIP:** These cabins look similar to first class with three seats per row, but there are fewer rows. The cabin is much smaller and less crowded so it is more quiet and spacious. More expensive than first class.

HARD SEAT FROM HARBIN

Harbin is a city in northern China mostly famous for being very, very cold. On top of regularly reaching temperatures of -60 degrees Fahrenheit, it is also one of China's most polluted cities. The downtown is split by a wide river frozen solid half the year, and the sky is so yellow with smog you can't see from one side of the river to the next. Looking out from the embankment into the thick mist, you get the eerie impression of being perched on the edge of the earth.

I visited this earthly paradise with my friend Tom in winter 2015. After spending a few days coughing and freezing our extremities, we regretfully made our way to the airport to catch a flight back to Beijing. Chaos greeted us at the departure terminal: the pollution was too thick for planes to fly, and all flights were cancelled until further notice. We fought our way through a mob of travelers for a chance to speak to the harried airline employee, who said the soonest she could rebook our flight for was in two days.

Tom needed to be in Beijing the next morning, so we decided to take the eighteen-hour train ride back. Unfortunately, everyone else had the same idea, and the only tickets available were standing tickets. I had my doubts about this idea but Tom was optimistic.

"It's okay," he assured me. "I've done this before. We buy a standing ticket, but once we are on the train we can go carriage to carriage and we will find some free seats or beds, I promise."

He was wrong, of course—the train attendants laughed in our faces when we asked if they had any free beds we could take. But Tom remained hopeful.

"These trains all have a dining carriage where you can sit at a table. We'll order dinner and sit there comfortably for a few hours. Just follow me!"

We walked along the train until we reached the dining area. We opened the door and a hundred faces turned to us. Each bore a smug smile that seemed to say, "Too slow, suckers." Every available surface already had three people stacked on it. We were directed outside with the other bumpkins who lost this round of musical chairs.

We stood at the junction between the train carriages. In this spot we could clearly feel the movement of the train beneath our feet. A draft brought in the frigid night air, and the occasional bump in the tracks would cause shards of frost to fall from above. We were surrounded by a crowd of men who eyed

(continued)

us curiously as they smoked their pungent Chinese cigarettes. After twenty minutes we knew we had to find a better solution.

We snuck into a soft sleeper carriage and plotted our next move. I thought we should bribe the carriage attendant to find us a free bed, but this plan was aborted when we realized between the two of us we barely had enough cash to buy a pack of chips. Tom suggested I use my feminine wiles to convince the attendant to help us. After much debate I sidled up to a young uniformed railway employee and awkwardly said hello. He frowned, asked to see my ticket, told me I was in the wrong carriage and escorted me out.

After my short-lived career as a modern-day Mata Hari, we decided the only solution was to drown our pain in alcohol until we arrived in Beijing. We wedged ourselves against the wall) outside the dining carriage and ordered a bottle of Er Tuo baijiu. Baijiu is China's national liquor and Er Tuo is the most common brand. Its business model is based on being cheap enough that any armless beggar can afford it, and strong enough to make said beggar fast forget the misery of his existence. The waitress clearly thought we must be in dire straits if we had fallen so low as to drink Er Tuo, and, taking pity on us, she allowed us to sit on top of a trash can by the train's kitchen.

The sight of two foreigners getting drunk on top of a trash can turned out to be a popular attraction on the train. For the next several hours we were visited by the kitchen staff and various passengers, who would ask what we were doing, encourage us to take a shot, and take a picture with us. The details of the night are hazy, but we woke up on the floor several hours later, lying in smelly liquid of an unknown origin, wearing a coat that did not belong to us as a blanket. By that point we were only a few hours from Beijing, and the kitchen staff, who had become our fast friends over the course of the night, offered us breakfast and gave us back our coveted seat on top of the trash can. We whiled away the rest of the ride fielding the usual questions about our impression of China, our impression of Chinese food, our romantic impressions of Chinese men and women, and how much money we made.

To this day Tom and I agree that our journey by standing ticket was one of the highlights of our China travels, and something we will never do again.

For regular trains:

- **Hard seat:** This is the most common kind of seat in regular trains. There are five seats per row, three on one side and two on the other. As the name implies, the seats are hard and uncomfortable and cannot be reclined. There are small tables between every two opposing rows. These are the cheapest rail travel option in China and cabins are correspondingly very crowded and dirty.

- **Soft seat:** These are available on only a few regular train journeys. They are similar to second class seats on the bullet trains, a little softer and more comfortable than hard seats. You get more space as there are only two seats on each side of the cabin. They cost 1.5x the price of a hard seat.

- **Standing tickets:** These are sold only during peak travel times when hard seats have run out. They entitle you to board the train where you will have to stand or find a spot on the floor that doesn't inconvenience anyone. Sometimes travelers buy standing tickets out of desperation or a misplaced sense of adventure. For short trips this might be tolerable, but before you buy a standing ticket for a long-distance journey, picture yourself sitting in dirt and unidentifiable liquids for eighteen hours, surrounded by bored Chinese men chain-smoking while little children run around screaming loudly and everyone blares awful Chinese pop music at full volume on grainy music speakers. If that doesn't appeal, avoid the standing tickets.

- **A tip if you decide to buy a standing ticket:** Arrive far in advance of the beginning of your journey so you can be one of the first in line to board the train. Immediately head to the canteen. You can sit at the tables there for the entire trip if you buy a meal—no one will force you to leave once you're done. All Chinese people know this so it's a sort of game of magical chairs when the train opens its doors and everyone rushes to secure a coveted seat in the cafeteria.

Sleeper Tickets

- **Hard sleepers** are packed six beds in a room, with three beds stacked on top of each other on each side. They can get a little loud at night, especially since many Chinese people have not yet learned to appreciate the communal benefits of wearing headphones. The cabins are usually filled with the sound of grainy traditional music and soap operas being played through tinny phone speakers. Nevertheless, they are quite comfortable if a little cramped. You are provided with a bed and a blanket.

- **Soft sleeper** is similar to hard sleeper but only four beds per room, two on each side, and the rooms are equipped with doors, which afford a little more privacy. The beds have a wider berth and more space to sit up straight.

- **Luxury sleepers** have two beds per cabin, stacked on top of each other on one side. The other side has a sofa and a resting area, and you have access to a private Western-style bathroom (no squatting!). These are twice the price of soft sleepers.

Food is served on the train, both in a canteen that serves regular Chinese dishes and through a trolley that offers Chinese snack favorites like instant noodles, spicy duck neck and preserved chicken feet.

Typical Prices for Popular Train Journeys

Journey	Bullet train 1st class	Bullet train 2nd class	Regular Hard sleeper	Regular Soft sleeper
Beijing-Shanghai	RMB 933 ($81)	RMB 531 ($81)	RMB 327 ($51)	RMB 499 ($73)
Beijing-Guilin/ Nanning	RMB 1250 ($184)	RMB 806 ($119)	RMB 499 ($71)	RMB 770 ($113)
Shanghai-Guangzhou	RMB 1179 ($198)	RMB 768 ($129)	RMB 418 ($70)	RMB 642 ($108)
Beijing-Xian	RMB 826 ($124)	RMB 517 ($78)	RMB 290 ($40)	RMB 442 ($62)
Beijing-Lhasa (Tibet)	N/A	N/A	RMB 766 ($115)	RMB 1,189 ($178)

How to Read Train Numbers

The first letter of each train number tells you what kind of train it is. Here is a guide to understanding the code:

Bullet Trains

- **G:** high-speed (300km/h). For long journeys between major cities.

- **D:** Electric multiple units (EMU) (250km/h). For medium to long distance journeys, sometimes offer overnight tickets.

- **C:** Intercity EMU (200 km/h). For shorter trips between neighboring cities.

Regular Trains

- **Z:** Direct express (160 km/h). Run nonstop between destinations.

- **T:** Express (140 km/h). Few stops between destinations.

- **K:** Fast (120 km/h). Several stops at large or mid-sized cities.

- **Ordinary fast:** (120 km/h) first four digits will begin with 1, 2, 4, or 5. These trains will make frequent stops on the journey.

- **Ordinary:** (100 km/h) first four digits will begin with 6, 7, 8, or 9. These trains will stop at almost every station along the way.

- **L:** (100 km/h) These are seasonal journeys that only operate during busy travel periods, usually national holidays.
- **Y:** (100 km/h) These journeys are also open only during peak travel times. Y trains stop only at major tourist destinations.
- **S:** (100 km/h) These short-distance trains connect major cities with their neighboring suburbs.

How to Buy a Train Ticket

It is advisable to buy your train tickets at least a couple weeks in advance if you want to avoid having to pay for first class after all the other options are sold out. You can buy tickets in person at the railway station up to sixty days ahead of time.

There are a couple exceptions:

- **D overnight trains** can only be bought 20 days in advance.
- **A few C tickets (e.g., Chengdu-Leshan)** can only be bought ten days in advance.

To board a train in China you will need your passport. The only exception is if your passport is currently in the hands of the police to update your visa, in which case you will need to show the yellow receipt paper from the police station. When you buy your ticket you will have to enter your name and information exactly as it appears on your passport or you will be refused entry on the train.

Buy a Ticket Online

- **www.12306.cn** is the official centralized source of all railway tickets in China. To buy a ticket here you need a Chinese bank card and the ability to navigate a Chinese website. This is usually the cheapest option as you are getting tickets directly from the source, so you don't pay a middleman's fee. If you are uncomfortable navigating a Mandarin website, here are detailed step-by-step instructions in English: www.travelchinacheaper.com/12306

- **WeChat Wallet:** Perhaps the fastest and most convenient way to buy a ticket is through WeChat. Open up your WeChat Wallet and scroll down until you see the "Rail and Flight" button. Clicking on the button will redirect you to a booking website. From there you will have to navigate the process in Mandarin, so get a Chinese friend to help you if you can't figure it out on your own.

- **China Highlights:** If Mandarin websites are too difficult for you to navigate, China Highlights lets you conduct the process entirely in English. They charge a fee of $6. www.chinahighlights.com/china-trains

If you book your ticket online, you will need to collect it at the train station before your journey. It's a good idea to arrive an hour before you leave as lines can sometimes be long. Show up at any counter indicated with "Ticket collection" (there will usually be an English sign) and present your passport and e-ticket number.

COUCHSURFING IN CHINA

After my first year in China I planned to take a solo trip to Hainan, a tropical island in the South China Sea. There were no hostels in Sanya, Hainan's capital, so in order to save money I decided to try Couchsurfing.

I picked a hostess who had dozens of glowing reviews on her website. Her waterfront hotel was called Tiannan Inn, and the owner, Ella, let foreigners stay there for free as a way to practice her English.

I went to Sanya hoping for a break from the bustle of Beijing, and Tiannan Inn was the perfect choice. It was beautiful, tucked away in a small corner of a peaceful hamlet bordering the beach. This type of village is dying out in Sanya as the government works to turn the city into a major tourist hub. Just across the road from the village I could see the future of the city: soulless resort hotels and deserted streets.

The village around the inn was a relic of the old Sanya, a communal town where shirtless men sat around low tables outside smoking, chatting, and drinking tea, while chickens, dogs and pigs wandered the streets and the smell of frying fish and meat perfumed the air. The village was dying when

I went; there were piles of rubble where houses once stood. Ella told me she feared her inn would soon go the same route as the government chased the locals off the land in order to develop more properties. She was right: A year later I asked if I could come back, and she told me the inn was gone.

Ella was a perfect hostess — warm, intelligent, and attentive. She invited me to share a bunk bed with her and her pregnant cat and insisted I eat every meal at her table for free. During the day she took me to her favorite swimming spots, and together we would swim far off the coast until we could barely see the beach. At night she invited me to drink warm beers and play guitar with the hotel staff as they told me about how Sanya had changed over the past decade.

The Inn attracted a variety of Chinese guests for dinner and for overnight stays — club owners from Shanghai, a middle class couple on their honeymoon, and members of the Chinese Navy working on a base nearby. In typical Chinese manner, they were curious about the foreigner and eager for the chance to talk to me. Every night I was invited to eat a feast of seafood and plied with baijiu until I could barely stumble up the bunk bed.

(continued)

My time at Tiannan Inn is one of my fondest memories in China. I particularly remember the Navy sailors (men and women) I met who treated me with such generosity — given their work and location I don't doubt they were working on issues pertaining to the South China Sea Islands. As our countries' leaders bluster about starting a war over the contested Islands, I hope the sailors remember me too. I like to think I showed them that Americans are not all greedy imperialist pigs, but normal people just trying to get through life preferably without suffering through nuclear Armageddon.

Buy a ticket in person

If for some reason you prefer not to book online, you can also buy tickets in person, either at the station or through an agency.

At the station

Buying a ticket at the station in China is the same as doing it in most places in the West: Find the ticket window, state your destination, present your passport, and pay.

Differences:

- The lines are very long. Expect to wait up to an hour to buy your ticket. By then it might be sold out — there will be a screen on the wall updating how many tickets are left for each journey, but you will have to read Chinese to understand

- Popular tickets sell out online before they can be bought at a station. If you are looking to take a train during peak travel time, you will have to buy it online

- It is very unlikely that the staff will be able to speak English. A few of China's biggest train stations (Beijing Railway Station, Shanghai Railway Station) will have a kiosk specifically for foreigners, but those are rare. If you struggle with Mandarin, ask a Chinese friend to help you write a note to take with you with the following information: train number (or departure city and destination), travel date, departure time, and seat class.

Through an agency

You can also book a ticket through a local agency. Many Chinese people do this to avoid the crowds and hassle of booking at the ticket agency in a train station. Agencies usually charge 5RMB for their services. They are open during regular working hours, so 8 A.M. to 5 P.M. It is highly unlikely the staff can speak English, so don't forget to bring a Chinese note if you need it.

Through a hotel or travel agency

Many hotels and travel agencies will offer to book your ticket for you. They will, however, charge a high service fee. This might be worth it for the convenience of dealing with English speakers and avoiding waiting in line.

Plane

China is the third-largest country in the world after Russia and Canada. It can take up to 40 hours to traverse its length by train. If you want to take a long journey in limited time (for example, take a trip to Tibet for a few days), I would advise taking a plane.

Delays

Be warned that every single one of your domestic flights will be delayed or cancelled. This is not a joke or exaggeration, it's a fact. Neither I nor anyone I know has ever boarded a flight on time in China. Reasons for delays run from pollution to rain to the pilot taking a nap. So if you choose to take a domestic flight, make sure you don't schedule anything important a day after you expect to leave or arrive because there is a high likelihood you will not be able to make it.

Major Chinese Airlines

- China Southern Airlines: www.csair.com
- China Eastern Airlines: en.ceair.com

- Air China (not to be confused with Taiwan's China Air): www.airchina.com.cn

You can book your flight directly on the airlines' website (look in the upper right corner for the "English" button). In order to find the cheapest flights, first go to www.kayak. com to see what your options are. Once you've found the flight number and airline, go to the company website and book it yourself.

If you prefer not to book online, you can also find a travel agency that will book for you. These charge a fee for their service, but they will also help you find the cheapest flight. Alternatively, you can go directly to the airport and find the airlines' ticket kiosk. They usually speak some English, but just in case you should bring a Chinese note explaining your travel plans.

Travel by Bus

Foreigners don't typically travel by bus around China since trains are cheap and quick. But there are some advantages to traveling by bus:

If you are on a strict budget, buses are the cheapest travel option.

Buses run more frequently than either planes or trains. In general you can expect a bus to a major city to take off every 20-30 minutes.

Since buses are so frequent, tickets run out more slowly than for planes and trains. You can buy a ticket the day before or even the day of, which is not the case for other methods of transportation.

The cheap cost of buses comes at a price, however—they tend to attract the poorest Chinese who are a bit rough around the edge. You can expect buses to be crowded and filled with cigarette smoke and the chatter of loud, rowdy locals. Many of the buses will already have been worn down by a hard lifetime of use by the time you step on them. They are frequently delayed for hours, sometimes because they break down, other times because they get stuck in China's nightmarish traffic jams.

Types of buses

- **Seated:** This is a regular bus with rows of seats facing forward. There are four seats per row, and legroom is ample enough for all but the most exceptionally tall.
- **Sleeper:** You can also buy an overnight sleeper bus, which comes with beds instead of seats. There are usually three rows of bunk beds with two aisles in between. You might have to scrunch up a little if you are short, because the beds are not very long. The top bunk is more expensive than the bottom (it's considered more peaceful and private).

How to buy a ticket

Unfortunately, it is not possible to buy bus tickets online, so you will have to buy one at the station yourself. Some hotels will also buy them for you at a fee. It is also difficult to find a bus schedule online—if you can write Mandarin you can try searching on Baidu for "[departure city] to [destination] bus schedule." Sometimes you will get results, although they might be outdated. But if you are traveling to a medium-sized or large city, usually there will be buses running every twenty or thirty minutes.

Chinese bus stations can be a little confusing—many cities have different bus stations based on the destination (there will be one bus station for journeys heading north, another for buses heading south, and so on). There are also different bus stations for long-distance and short-distance buses. In order to find which station you will need to go to, you can consult an updated China travel guide, ask at a hotel, or ask your taxi driver (if you tell him your destination he will often know which bus station to take you to).

Once you are at the bus station, find the ticket counter. Lines are typically shorter than in train stations, but again the staff is unlikely to speak English. There will be a schedule on the wall or in LED lights on a board, but you will have to be able to read Mandarin to understand it. If you don't know Mandarin, write a note in Chinese with your destination and the kind of bus you want to take (seater or sleeper), and the service person will be able to help you.

CHINESE TOUR GROUPS

A co-worker invited me to join her on a weekend trip to Inner Mongolia as part of a Chinese tour group.

The most striking characteristic about Chinese tour groups is how communal they are—there is a strong emphasis on continuously playing games and singing together to build group cohesiveness, and a view that everyone must do everything together or you are being anti-social. As an individualist American I found this atmosphere stifling, but the upside is that everyone feels included and welcome.

Our group comprised about 50 Beijing office workers and their children. The main attraction of the trip was a 10K hike through Jade Dragon Desert. The path we took was much more dangerous than I expected. We were climbing on narrow ledges of massive boulders with a steep fall onto sharp rocks if our feet slipped. The children were climbing everywhere like monkeys, their parents either unaware or unconcerned that they were one loose stone away from breaking their necks. If a tour group in a Western country tried to take a group of untrained tourists on a hike like that they would be out of business before they could say "negligence lawsuit."

We crawled along with frequent stops to let every-one catch up. The tour guide would pause the group every two hours so we could play games and sing songs. This quickly became tiresome so I walked ahead of the group with an extremely fit Chinese banker, who valiantly tried to explain to me in Mandarin the woes of the Chinese economy, despite my frequent blank stares and requests for clarification.

At the end of the day we were taken to eat a feast of Mongolian food. It was rich in sizzling meats, fats, and dairy, more suited for the army of Genghis Khan coming back from a day of raping and pillaging than office workers on holiday.

Our guide bought a bottle of the local baijiu. When the Chinese break out the baijiu you know the night is going to be wild. As the lone foreigner, I was singled out repeatedly for toasts and made to drink more than anyone else (which isn't saying much, since they were all Chinese). The night ended with everyone dancing and singing Beijing opera.

The Chinese men seemed very happy to be talk-ing to a foreign girl and all promised me they would take care of me for the rest of the trip, whatever that meant. Then they sent me pictures and videos that they had been surreptitiously taking of me all day.

(continued)

In a Western country this would be creepy stalker-ish behavior, but coming from Chinese men it was sort of sweet.

The next day we piled on the bus back to Beijing. After our night of baijiu the ice was broken, and for the ten-hour ride back the tour guide made us all take turns to stand up and sing. At first they tried to single me out more than anyone else, but they soon realized it wasn't false modesty that made me say if I sang for too long their ears would start bleeding, and I was left in peace. It was a nice weekend, but the constant insistence on singing and playing games made me feel like I was back in kindergarten, and it was my last group travel in China.

As for all travel in China, you will need your passport to buy your ticket and board the bus. There usually aren't any electric outlets on Chinese buses, so bring your own portable charger. Buses stop every couple hours at rest stations where you can use the bathroom and buy some food, but don't expect any Michelin restaurants. If you are a picky eater, bring food with you. If there are no convenient rest stations, buses will sometimes stop on the side of the road and everyone will use the fields nearby as their toilet. Bus travel in China is a bit rough but that adds to the adventure!

Travel Companies

A popular option for both Chinese and expats is to book with a local travel company for weekend trips. These tend to be very cheap—expect to pay something like RMB 400 ($60) for three days of traveling, including transportation, hotel, activities, and three meals a day. Because of the price, don't expect any luxury hotel accommodations. But the rooms will generally be clean-ish and the food will be good. It is unlikely there will be many people who can speak English, however—either go with friends or expect to spend a few days practicing your Mandarin.

China is a communal country, and people like to take part in group activities. On the one hand this can be a fun way for you to communicate with locals and experience Chinese culture. They will be very curious about the foreigner and will try to practice their English with you. (Usually this means the bravest among them will say, "Hello, how are you?" and then everyone will dissolve in giggles as if watching a Chinese person speak with a foreigner is the funniest thing imaginable.)

On the other hand, these tours are rigidly scheduled and don't leave much flexibility for you to do anything by yourself. You will probably be made to sing and play games with the other guests in the group. Chinese people love singing and are not shy about doing it in public, which takes some getting used to, but it's fun once you get over your initial self-consciousness. If you are the only foreigner, expect to be singled out continuously and made to sing for everyone.

Driving in China

You cannot legally drive in China without a Chinese driver's license. If you have a International Driving Permit, you will need to go through an additional examination to get it converted into a Chinese license.

Provisional driver's licenses are available without any additional driving tests, but these last a maximum of three months. If you are under a long-term visa (one year or more work visa), you are not eligible for a provisional driver's license.

How to get a provisional Chinese driver's license

You will need a driver's license from your native country and an international driver's permit

- Have your driver's license from back home translated into Mandarin through a government-approved translation service

- Make sure you are registered at the local police station of the city where you reside. You should have done this when you rented an apartment, as it is the law for all foreigners to register at the local police station. You will need to have proof of this registration to bring to the DMV with you.

- Head to the DMV (车管所) of your city. You will need to bring three one-inch photos with you (or have some made at the station for 30 RMB). You will need to fill out some forms and have your eyes checked. If you complete all these hurdles, congratulations, you now have a provisional driver's license!

How to get a Chinese driver's license if you already have a driver's license at home

You will need your home country's driver's license (translated into Chinese through a government-approved translation service), a residence permit with at least three months validity, your passport, a medical certificate, and three one-inch photos.

Head to your city's DMV (车管所), where you will present all your documents. If you have all the necessary documentation, you will be eligible to take a written test.

The written test consists of 100 questions (in English). You need to get at least 90 percent correct to pass the test. If you fail twice, you will have to wait twenty days before you can try again.

The website www.chinesedrivingtest.com allows you to practice for the Chinese driving test, so you have some idea what to expect.

China Drive is another app that lets you take practice exams for the test in English.

How to get a Chinese driver's license if you don't have a license at home

If you are over 18 years old and are a legal resident of China, you have the right to a Chinese driver's license even if you don't have a license back home.

You will need your passport, a residence permit with at least three months validity, a medical certificate, and three one-inch photos.

You will have to pass three exams. You are allowed to fail once with no penalty; if you fail twice you will have to repay the fee and wait twenty days to retake the exam.

- The written exam (100 questions)
- Basic driving and parking skills test on a track
- Driving test in city traffic
- Another written exam on correct driving habits (50 questions)

You are also required to sign up for driving school before taking the exam. There are driving schools that accept foreigners, even some targeted specifically at expats. Expect the school to last two to three months and cost RMB 3,000-8,000 ($450-1,200).

Renting a car

Once you have either a provisional or a regular Chinese driver's license, you are eligible to rent a car. Most Chinese cities have many car rental shops. The deposit will be RMB 2,000-15,000 ($250-2000). Renting a car by the day costs 100-1,000 RMB depending on the car ($15-150). Prices rise during weekends and holidays, so the cheapest time to rent is Monday-Thursday. The price includes car insurance. You can rent for one day up to a year — the longer you rent, the cheaper the price. Once you have your car you are free to roam around China, but keep in mind that China has twice as many fatal road accidents per year as the United States despite having only half as many cars on the road. Be careful out there!

A note on traveling to Tibet

If you look at this map of China you will notice that most of the country's 1.4 billion people are crammed into the eastern half of the country, and the rest is mostly deserts and mountains.

The two Western-most provinces are Xinjiang and Tibet. They are famous for their stunning, rugged landscapes, colorful ethnic minorities, and violent civil unrest. Both the Uyghurs (the native Muslim people of Xinjiang) and the Tibetans have been seeking independence from Beijing for decades.

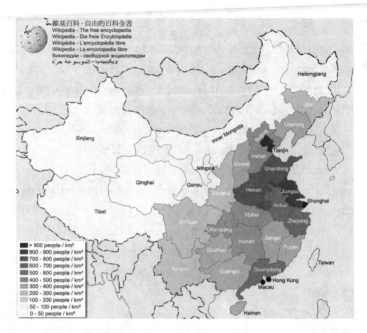

維基百科 · 自由的百科全書
Wikipedia - The free encyclopedia
Wikipédia - Die freie Enzyklopädie
Wikipédia - L'encyclopédie libre
Wikipedia - La enciclopedia libre
Википедии - свободной энциклопедии
ويكيبيديا - الموسوعة حرة

> 900 people / km²
800 - 900 people / km²
700 - 800 people / km²
600 - 700 people / km²
500 - 600 people / km²
400 - 500 people / km²
300 - 400 people / km²
200 - 300 people / km²
100 - 200 people / km²
50 - 100 people / km²
0 - 50 people / km²

China population density map

The natural beauty and unique culture of Tibet attract the interest of tourists, yet there are strict limits on foreigners traveling there. **If you wish to travel to China, it is advisable not to put either of these provinces on your proposed itinerary as this could be grounds for rejecting your application.** Once you have a Chinese visa you can travel to Xinjiang freely, but be aware that there are some safety concerns regarding radical Muslim independence movements.

A foreigner traveling to Tibet must have a tour guide that provides travel permits, a private car, and a driver. There are no exceptions to this rule. Foreigners are forbidden to travel in Tibet unaccompanied. You can find a travel company online or in any major Chinese city and they will obtain the special permit for you (it is called the Tibet Travel Permit, issued by the Tibet Tourism Bureau).

If you are on a tourist visa you should be able to obtain the travel permit within five working days as long as you fill out a form and send copies of your passport and visa.

If you are on a Z visa (working) you will additionally need to provide your residence permit and a certificate from your place of employment on official company letterhead with your name, passport number, and an official company stamp.

If you are on a F visa (business) you will need a certification letter from your travel agency.

If you are on a student visa you are NOT permitted to travel to Tibet, and your request for a Tibet Travel Permit will consequently be denied.

Your departure airport or train station will check to make sure you have a **Tibet Travel Permit** before you can board. Once you are in Tibet, you will also need to apply for an **Aliens' Travel Permit**. This can be done only from within Tibet. If you wish to visit particularly sensitive zones, you might also need to apply for a **Military Permit.** These will generally be checked only in hotels, though you must be prepared to provide them upon request at any time.

Costs

Tibet Travel Permits are technically free, but every travel agency will charge you to obtain one. Expect to pay between 350 and 700 RMB

Tour guides generally charge around 250-300 RMB per day. This is a group cost, not individual.

Vehicles are the most expensive cost you will incur on your trip. The price of vehicle rentals depends on distance traveled and time of year, but here is a general idea of what you can expect to pay during high season:

- Lhasa → Nam Tso Lake → Lhasa: 3000 RMB to 4000 RMB
- Lhasa → Yamdrok Lake → Gyantse → Shigatse → Sakya → Everest Base Camp → Nepal Border: 11,000 RMB to 15,000 RMB
- Lhasa → Yamdrok Lake → Gyantse → Shigatse → Sakya → Everest Base Camp → Lhasa: 10,000 RMB to 14,000 RMB
- Lhasa → Tidrum Nunnery → Drugung Monastery → Samye Monastery → Lhasa: 7500 RMB to 9000 RMB
- Lhasa → Samye → Tsetang → Yumbulhagang → Mindroling → Lhasa: 7200 RMB to 8800 RMB
- Lhasa → Shigatse → Saga → Lake Manasarovar → Mt. Kailash trek → Lhasa: 22,000 RMB to 25,000 RMB
- Lhasa → Shigatse → Saga → Manasarovar → Mt. Kailash trek → Guge Kingdom → Ali → Lhasa: 25,000 RMB to 28,000 RMB

Again, this is a group cost, not individual.

Reputable travel agencies to organize your Tibet trip:

- www.windhorseadventuretours.com
- www.visittibet.com
- www.khampacaravan.com

INTERNATIONAL TRAVEL

China is a good base for other travels around Asia. Flight tickets to Thailand, Malaysia, Vietnam, and elsewhere are quite low. If you book in advance, expect to pay about 3,000-5,000 RMB ($450-750) for a return ticket to a Southeast Asian country. Korea and Japan are more expensive—expect to pay 6,000 RMB ($900) for a return ticket to Tokyo or Seoul.

If you plan to travel during Chinese national holidays, always remember to book your tickets far in advance or prices will skyrocket. You can book flights through any of the popular Chinese websites mentioned above, or an international company (just stay away from Air Malaysia!)

International flights are much more reliable than domestic flights, and it is no more likely that your international flight from Beijing will be delayed than your flights from the US.

Photo Credits

page xxviii: Original photo by Nicholas Kenrick www.flickr.com/photos/33363480@N05

page 32: Original photo by Ashley Wang. www.flickr.com/photos/ashley-rly/

page 62: Original image by Robert Ennals www.flickr.com/photos/robennals/

page 101: Original image by Fernando Frazão/Agência Brasil. agenciabrasil.ebc.com.br/rio-2016/foto/2016-08/michael-phelps-conquista-20a-medalha-de-ouro-e-e-ovacionado

page 113: Original photo by Marc van der Chijs. www.flickr.com/photos/chijs/

page 117: Modified image by Roman Boed www.flickr.com/photos/romanboed/33399544191

page 118: Original image by Morio commons.wikimedia.org/wiki/File:Sanlitun_2015_October.jpg

page 132: Original image by Dick Thomas Johnson www.flickr.com/photos/31029865@N06/6554188007

page 167: Image by 維基小霸王 commons.wikimedia.org/wiki/File:West_Gate_of_Peking_University.jpg

page 197: Original photo by Antoine Taveneaux commons.wikimedia.org/wiki/File:Niujie_Mosque.jpg

page 262: Image by Sadhanakere commons.wikimedia.org/wiki/File:Population_density_of_China_by_first-level_administrative_regionsEnglish.png

Acknowledgments

I would like to thank a few people for their support throughout this project. My friend Rose Wang, without whom my China adventure would never have happened. My agent Barbara Braun, my publisher Travelers' Tales and editor Larry Habegger for taking a chance on an unknown writer. And of course my dear father, without whose editorial skills, unwavering support, and saintly patience this book would never have become a reality.

About the Author

A few months after her twenty-first birthday and shortly after graduating with an unmarketable degree in history, Sophia Erickson was waiting tables in rural Massachusetts and contemplating years of student loan servitude. After a chance email exchange with an old friend she booked a one-way ticket to Beijing where she spent the following two years. A graduate of Oxford University and Phillips Academy, Sophia now resides in the Middle East. You can find out more about her at www.sophiaerickson.com or contact her directly at writerickson@gmail.com.